Brainfluence

100 WAYS TO PERSUADE AND CONVINCE CONSUMERS WITH NEUROMARKETING

ROGER DOOLEY

WILEY

John Wiley & Sons, Inc.

Published by John Wiley & Sons, Inc., Hoboken, New Jersey.
Published simultaneously in Canada.

For general information on our other products and services or for technical support, please contact our Customer Care Department within the United States at (800) 762-2974, outside the United States at (317) 572-3993 or fax (317) 572-4002.

Wiley publishes in a variety of print and electronic formats and by print-on-demand. Some material included with standard print versions of this book may not be included in e-books or in print-on-demand. If this book refers to media such as a CD or DVD that is not included in the version you purchased, you may download this material at http://booksupport.wiley.com. For more information about Wiley products, visit www.wiley.com.

Library of Congress Cataloging-in-Publication Data:

Dooley, Roger, 1952-
    Brainfluence : 100 ways to persuade and convince consumers with neuromarketing / Roger Dooley.
        p. cm
    ISBN 978-1-118-11336-3 (hardback); ISBN 978-1-118-17594-1 (ebk);
    ISBN 978-1-118-17595-8 (ebk); ISBN 978-1-118-17596-5 (ebk)
        1. Neuromarketing.   2. Marketing—Psychological aspects.
        3. Advertising—Psychological aspects.   4. Consumers—Psychology.   I. Title.
    HF5415.12615.D66   2012
    658.8001'9—dc23
                                                                        2011029938

Printed in the United States of America

10 9 8 7 6 5 4 3 2 1

To Carol, for putting up with me, and to my mother,
who sparked my interest in words

Contents

v

Preface

Why *Brainfluence?*

Today's #1 Challenge: Better Results With Less Money

In these trying economic times, marketers are being called upon to accomplish more, but with fewer resources. Conventional wisdom pairs sales success with the amount of resources you expend. If one out of four sales calls results in a sale, make twice as many calls to double sales. If 10 clicks on a search ad yield one inquiry, on average, then all it takes to up the lead flow is to keep buying more clicks. Need more brand awareness? Buy more ads, sponsor more events, or plaster your logo in more places.

The problem with the "more resources applied = more success" model is that it gets expensive—very expensive. Worst of all, if the cost of getting a sale isn't justified by the profit from that sale, the model breaks down completely. Applying more resources just results in bigger losses.

The Answer: Appealing to Your Customer's Brain

This book is all about *smarter* marketing. Although there are certainly many ways to boost the effectiveness of your marketing and sales efforts, in *Brainfluence* we'll follow one theme: *understanding how your customers' brains work to get better results with less money.*

From Ad Psychology to Neuromarketing

The idea of using our understanding of how people think in marketing and sales is hardly a new idea. No doubt, salespeople in ancient bazaars had some of the same insights into human nature that we have today. And for decades we've seen terms like *advertising psychology* and *sales psychology* thrown around in articles and books.

So what has changed since the era depicted in TV's *Mad Men?* One huge shift is the development of modern neuroscience. For all its accomplishments, traditional psychology treated the brain as a black box. Give a person a stimulus, and you get a response. Even more complex models of how we think (Freud's, for example) were based on observation, experiments, and deduction, but not on a detailed understanding of brain science.

Modern neuroscience has brought us tools that help us see inside our brains and open up psychology's black box. Now, with the magic of functional magnetic resonance imaging (fMRI) brain scans, we can see, for example, that our brain's response to a price that's too high is very much like getting pinched: it's painful. Electroencephalogram (EEG) technology is bringing the cost of measuring some kinds of brain activity down and allowing larger sample sizes for statistically reliable optimization of ads and products.

How Rational Are We?

We all like to think there are good reasons for what we do and that our decisions result from a conscious, deliberative process. Although certainly there are rational components to many of our decisions and actions, researchers are constantly exposing new ways in which our subconscious drives our choices, often with minimal conscious involvement.

Since the early days of their science, psychologists have suggested that our conscious minds are not in charge of what we do. Freud, for example, developed elaborate theories involving repression and dreams. Many modern scientists attribute behaviors to our evolutionary past. Even as we tweet from our iPhones, evolutionary psychologists say, our brains are operating with software from our hunter-gatherer days.

Not all the new insights come from complex neuroscientific studies. Around the world, behavioral researchers are conducting simple experiments with human subjects that reveal how our brains work and, in some cases, work much differently than we might predict. Duke University professor Dan Ariely is one of these researchers, and if you doubt the existence of unconscious influences on our decisions, read his engaging book, *Predictably Irrational*.

What Is Neuromarketing?

I've written the blog titled *Neuromarketing* since 2005, and I have explored many ways that marketers can use different aspects of brain science to improve results. There's no universal agreement as to exactly what does (and what doesn't) constitute neuromarketing. Some would use the term to refer only to brain scan–based marketing analysis. Others might add related technologies, such as biometrics (e.g., tracking heart rate and respiration) and eye tracking.

I prefer a broadly inclusive definition of neuromarketing that includes behavioral research and behavior-based strategies. To me, it's all a continuum; the reason the fMRI machine shows that your brain lights up at a particular point in a commercial is likely due to some underlying preference or "program." The brain scan can show you where the hot button is, but it can't change it or push it.

Neuromarketing is all about understanding how our brains work, regardless of the science used, and employing that understanding to improve both our marketing and our products.

Good or Evil?

Some people find the concept of neuromarketing frightening. They view it as manipulative and unethical. I disagree.

If neuromarketing techniques are used properly, we'll have better ads, better products, and happier customers. Who wouldn't want a product they liked more or a less boring commercial? Would consumers really be better off if companies annoyed them with ineffective but costly ad campaigns?

Any marketing tool can be "evil" if the company behind it misuses it. Advertising can be fun and informative; it can also contain false information or misrepresent the product. Warranties are a great consumer benefit, but not if the company fails to honor them. Neuromarketing is simply another technique that marketers can use to understand their customers and serve them better.

Most companies seek to build their brand for the long haul and won't abuse their customers with any kind of deception or manipulation, neuromarketing or otherwise.

What This Book Is Not

This isn't a science book or a neuroscience primer. It's not an attempt to explain the scientific basis for branding or advertising. (One book that does that in great detail is the excellent *The Branded Mind* by Erik du Plessis.) You won't find any brain diagrams, because I've kept the references to specific brain structures to a minimum. (And if you find an occasional reference to the amygdala or prefrontal cortex, don't worry; these won't be on the test, and you won't need to be able to pinpoint them on a brain chart!)

This isn't a big idea book. I love books like Chris Anderson's *Free* and Malcolm Gladwell's *Blink* that explore one trend or topic in great depth. For better or worse, *Brainfluence* isn't one of those. Instead, it's a compilation of a hundred smaller, bite-sized ideas, each one based on neuroscience or behavior research.

This is a book of practical advice for marketers, managers, and business owners, not scientists or neuroscience geeks. (If you *are* a scientist or neuroscience geek, I've included a reference for just about every study I mention; feel free to explore more deeply.)

Who Can Benefit From This Book

I've selected the hundred topics in *Brainfluence* to be applicable to a wide range of budgets and situations. Although some of the ideas in this book come from costly research using fMRI machines or other technology unavailable to most firms, each topic provides a marketing approach that is usable by any organization, often at low cost. Marketers in both large and small businesses will find problems like their own and solutions they can implement on a scale that fits their needs.

Each topic in *Brainfluence* is designed to describe research findings that show how our brains work and offer one or more ways to directly apply that knowledge to real-world marketing situations. Although I make a few leaps here and there in relating that research to actual business needs, you won't find me saying, "Do this because I'm telling you to."

Most of the book uses the language of business, talking about customers and sales, but many of the concepts are applicable to the nonprofit sector as well. Every nonprofit today has to accomplish more with fewer resources, and many of the topics here will enable them to do just that.

It isn't necessary to read this book from cover to cover, or even from front to back. Although the ideas are grouped in major categories, each topic stands on its own. Feel free to browse as you like.

And remember: "marketing smarter" doesn't just mean using *your* brain; it means using your *customer's* brain too!

Acknowledgments

It's customary to acknowledge the contributions of those who collaborated in writing the book. In creating both *Brainfluence* and my blog, *Neuromarketing*, my partners are the dedicated researchers who devote their lives to teasing out the details of how our brains work. Some of them I have met; others I know only via correspondence or their work. It's people like Dan Ariely, George Loewenstein, Robert Cialdini, Paul Zak, Read Montague, and so many others, who do the heavy lifting in this field. To them, thank you!

About the Author

Roger Dooley is founder of Dooley Direct LLC, a marketing consultancy, and author of the popular blog *Neuromarketing*. He cofounded College Confidential, the highest-traffic website for college-bound students, which was acquired by Hobsons, a unit of London-based DMGT, in 2008. He served as Vice President of Digital Marketing at Hobsons and remains in a consulting role to the firm. Dooley is a long-time entrepreneur and direct marketer.

Dooley holds an engineering degree from Carnegie Mellon University (1971) and an MBA from the University of Tennessee (1977). He resides in Austin, Texas.

1

Sell to 95 Percent of Your Customer's Brain

NINETY-FIVE PERCENT of our thoughts, emotions, and learning occur without our conscious awareness, according to Harvard marketing professor and author Gerald Zaltman.[1] And he's not the only expert who thinks this way; the 95 percent rule is used by many neuroscientists to estimate subconscious brain activity. (NeuroFocus founder and chief executive officer [CEO], A. K. Pradeep, estimates it at 99.999 percent in his book, *The Buying Brain*.[2]) It's doubtful we'll ever be able to arrive at a precise number, but all neuroscientists agree there's a lot going on under the surface in our brains. (There's debate, too, over the terminology; many scientists prefer *nonconscious* or *preconscious* for greater precision. I'll mostly use *subconscious*, simply because it's the most familiar term.)

One indication of the power of our subconscious comes from a study that showed that subjects given a puzzle to solve actually solved it as much as *eight seconds before they were consciously aware of having solved it*. (The researchers determined this by monitoring brain activity with an electroencephalograph (EEG) and identifying the pattern that correlated with reaching a solution.[3]) Other research shows a lag in decision making—our brains seem to reach a decision before we are consciously aware of it.

The realization that the vast majority of our behaviors are determined subconsciously is a basic premise of most of the strategies in this book, and indeed, of the entire field of neuromarketing. Customers

1

generally can't understand or accurately explain why they make choices in the marketplace, and efforts to tease out that information by asking them questions are mostly doomed to failure. Furthermore, marketing efforts based mostly on customer statements and self-reports of their experiences, preferences, and intentions are equally doomed.

Brainfluence Takeaway: Stop Selling to 5 Percent of Your Customer's Brain

The rest of the takeaways in this book are a lot more specific and actionable, but this one is the most important. Despite knowing that rational, conscious cognitive processes are a small influence in human decision making, we often focus most of our message on that narrow slice of our customer's thinking. We provide statistics, feature lists, cost/benefit analyses, and so on, while ignoring the vast emotional and nonverbal subconscious share of brain activity.

Although there are conscious and rational parts in most decisions, marketers need to focus first on appealing to the buyer's emotions and unconscious needs. It's not always bad to include factual details, as they will help the customer's logical brain justify the decision—just don't expect them to make the sale!

SECTION
One

Price and Product Brainfluence

EVERY MARKETER WRESTLES with decisions about how to structure a product line and how to set prices. A small difference in pricing can make a big difference in profits, but the wrong price can kill sales, too. Fortunately, neuromarketing has plenty to tell us about these closely related areas!

2

The "Ouch!" of Paying

ONE OF THE key insights neuroeconomics and neuromarketing research have provided us is that buying something can cause the pain center in our brain to light up. Researchers at Carnegie Mellon and Stanford universities presented subjects with cash, put them in a functional magnetic resonance imaging (fMRI) machine to record their brain activity, and then offered them items, each with a price. Some of the products were overpriced, and others were a good value. The subjects were able to choose to buy items with their money or keep the cash. The researchers compared self-reporting of purchase intentions by the subjects, brain scan data, and actual purchases.[1]

I spoke with Carnegie Mellon University professor George Loewenstein after that work was published, and he noted that one significant aspect of the findings is that the brain scans predicted buying behavior almost as well as the self-reported intentions of the subjects. In other words, absent any knowledge of what the subject intended to do, viewing the brain scan was just about as accurate as asking the subject what he or she would do.

Loewenstein pointed out that, in this experiment, the questions about the intentions of the subject were quite straightforward and one would expect the answers to be good predictors of actual behavior.

The "negative" activation produced by cost is relative, according to Loewenstein. That is, it isn't just the dollar amount; it's the context of

4

the transaction. Thus, people can spend hundreds of dollars on accessories when buying a car with little pain, but a vending machine that takes 75 cents and produces nothing is very aggravating.

Bundling Minimizes Pain

Auto luxury bundles minimize negative activation because their price tag covers multiple items. The consumer can't relate a specific price to each component in the bundle (leather seats, sunroof, etc.) and hence can't easily evaluate the fairness of the deal or whether the utility of the accessory is worth the price.

Fairness Counts

Cost isn't the only variable that causes "pain." It's really the perceived fairness or unfairness of the deal that creates the reaction. Other parts of an offer that caused it to appear unfair would presumably cause a similar reaction as a price that was too high.

There's not always a single "fair" price for an item. For most people, a fair price for a cup of coffee at Starbucks would likely be higher than a cup from a street corner coffee cart. A famous study by economist Richard Thaler showed that thirsty beachgoers would pay nearly twice as much for a beer from a resort hotel than for the same brew from a small, rundown grocery store.[2]

Credit as Painkiller

Overall, Loewenstein wasn't enthused about using his work for neuro-marketing purposes. He pointed out that, for many years, credit card companies have prospered while encouraging consumers to spend too much by exploiting the principles he's now uncovering in his research.

The problem is that, for many consumers, the credit card takes the pain (quite literally, from the standpoint of the customer's brain) out of purchasing. Pulling cash out of one's wallet causes one to evaluate the purchase more carefully.

We think this makes a lot of sense and is entirely consistent with real-world behavior. A credit card reduces the pain level by transferring the cost to a future period where it can be paid in small increments. Hence, not only does a credit card enable a consumer to buy something without actually having the cash, but it also tips the scale as one's brain weighs the pain versus the benefit of the purchase. This can be a bad combination for individuals lacking financial discipline.

Brainfluence Takeaway: Minimum Pain, Maximum Sales

Pricing and the product itself need to be optimized to minimize the pain of paying. First, the price must be seen as fair. If your product is more expensive than others, take the time to explain why it is a premium product.

If you find yourself in a situation where, for cost or other reasons, the price of a product is likely to produce an "ouch!" reaction from your customers, see if some kind of a bundle with complementary items will dull the pain.

Payment terms and credit options can also reduce the pain of paying. Don't push your customers into buying products they can't afford, but even affluent customers will feel less pain if they don't have to make immediate payment in cash.

3

Don't Sell Like a Sushi Chef

I LOVE SUSHI. But I hate the way most sushi restaurants sell it, with a separate price for each tiny piece. Every bite I take seems to have a price tag on it. "Mmm . . . not bad. But was that mouthful worth five bucks? Do I really want another one?"

It turns out my brain is normal, at least in relation to my aversion to the typical sushi pricing scheme. In the last chapter, we met Carnegie Mellon University economics and psychology professor George Loewenstein. Another insight from his work is that selling products in a way that the consumer sees the price increase with every bit of consumption causes the most pain. This isn't physical pain, of course, but rather activation of the same brain areas associated with physical pain. In an interview with *SmartMoney*, Loewenstein noted[3]:

> [Consumers are] not weighing the current gratification vs. future gratifications. They experience an immediate pang of pain [when they think of how much they have to pay for something] . . .

> It also explains why AOL switched from pay-per-hour Internet service to pay-per-month. When they did that, they got a flood of subscribers . . . Why do people love to prepay for things or pay a flat rate for things? Again, it mutes the pang of pain. The worst-case alternative is when you pay for sushi and you're paying per piece.

Or watching the taxi meter; you know how much every inch of the way is costing you.

Marketers have realized this for years, and they have responded with offers designed to minimize the pain associated with buying their products. All-inclusive meal options are popular at many eateries. Netflix crushed its video rental competitors in part by its "all-you-can-watch" price strategy. Cruises have surged in popularity in part because they deliver a vacation experience for a fixed price. In each case, the marketer offers a single, relatively attractive price that removes additional pain from the buying experience.

Paying for Pain Avoidance

In many situations, the single price is actually higher than the amount the consumer would have spent on individual food items, movie rentals, and so on. Nevertheless, the all-inclusive number is likely to appeal to many consumers, particularly those that Loewenstein would identify as being most sensitive to the pain of buying.

Brainfluence Takeaway: Avoid Multiple Pain Points

To minimize customer pain, marketers should always try to avoid multiple individual pain points in the purchasing process. Obviously, some situations make individual purchases unavoidable; for example, a grocery store can't offer fee-based shopping instead of item-by-item pricing.

Many business situations, though, will permit some experimentation with a single-price approach for items usually purchased separately, such as a monthly or annual fee instead of individual transactions. That simpler pricing approach may boost not only sales, but because some people will pay a premium for pain avoidance, profit margins as well.

4

Picturing Money

THE CONCEPT OF *priming* is simple, although it's also a bit unsettling: if you present an individual with subtle cues, you can affect that person's subsequent behavior, even though he or she is entirely unaware of either the priming or behavioral changes. Money-related images are some of the more potent forms of priming.

Psychologist Kathleen Vohs has studied priming extensively and found that supplying subjects with cues related to money increases selfish behavior. For example, she and her colleagues had student subjects either read an essay that mentioned money or sit facing a poster that pictured different types of currency.

The subjects who were primed with money cues took 70 percent longer to ask for help in solving a difficult problem and spent only half as much time helping another person (who, unknown to the subject, was actually part of the experiment) needing assistance.

The money-primed subjects also preferred to work alone and chose solitary leisure activities compared with unprimed subjects. They even sat farther apart when setting up chairs to chat with another subject.

Vohs concludes that even subtle money cues change the frame of mind people are in: they don't want to depend on others, nor do they want others to depend on them.

This work has interesting implications for advertisers who frequently use money themes in their ads. Big savings, higher investment returns, visions of prosperous retirement, money containers ranging from piggy banks to gleaming bank vaults . . . ads are full of these images. Most of these ads appeal to the selfish interest of the viewer, so any priming that takes place matches the intent of the advertisement. A mutual fund company touting superior returns and prosperous-looking retirees clearly wants to appeal to the self-interest of the customer; the company hopes the viewer will be sufficiently enticed by these images to transfer funds to it.

Money-related advertising images are pervasive in other types of ads, though, and not all appeal to selfish interests. Many print, television, and even in-store ads seem to emphasize savings. Are "save money on gifts for Mom" advertisers shooting themselves in the foot by subtly priming the would-be gift givers with selfish feelings?

The advertisers who should be particularly cautious about money cues are those who want to appeal to the viewer's feelings about others. Filling viewers with feelings of warmth and a desire to please someone else, and then reminding them about money, could be self-defeating.

Really, of course, it's a trade-off. Good salespeople often make the sale using feelings and emotion, and then close the deal with a financial incentive that has an expiration looming. If you've ever sat through a time-share sales pitch, you'll recognize that technique. Much of the pitch is intended to evoke warm feelings about recreation, quality time with family and friends, and so on, but there's always a financial incentive as the close approaches. Special financing is available only today, there's a price reduction for 48 hours, and so on. This approach is clearly effective. An advertiser must make a judgment call on whether and how to bring money into the picture if the appeal is primarily an emotional one.

No Money in Sight

Think about the long-running A Diamond Is Forever campaign. This is a good example of advertising that scrupulously avoids introducing money cues. Their ads target the luxury gift market. Spending large sums of money to give someone else a polished piece of carbon whose value is determined by cartel-enforced scarcity is hardly a concept that appeals to one's self-interest.

This effective ad campaign is a purely emotional pitch that would be spoiled by a tagline that offered, for example, "special savings in December!" The ads even avoid talking about the investment value of diamonds.

Restaurant Lessons

Even a simple currency symbol in front of a price can make a difference. One Cornell study looked at several common restaurant price display techniques:

Numerical with dollar sign: $12.00

Numerical without dollar sign or decimals: 12

Spelled out: twelve dollars

The researchers expected that the written/scripted prices would perform best, but they found that the guests with the simple numeral prices (those without dollar signs or decimals) spent significantly more than the other two groups did. When you visit a restaurant and find the menu has small prices presented this way, you'll know they are up on their neuromarketing best practices![4]

Brainfluence Takeaway: Use Money Cues Wisely

Use currency symbols in ads for products consistent with selfish feelings—products that offer financial independence, for example, or even a self-indulgent purchase like a sports car.

For campaigns focused on giving and thinking about others, such as gifts, nonprofit appeals, and so forth, advertisers may want to be a bit cautious and should likely avoid introducing financial imagery.

5

Anchors Aweigh!

HERE'S A SCENARIO: You decide to venture into a cell phone store (despite your reluctance to deal with a bewildering number of phones, options, plans, and confusing pricing). As usual, you find you'll have to wait a bit for a salesperson. The greeter hands you a card with a big "97" printed on it and says, "It should only be a few minutes. We'll call your number, 97, when a salesperson can help you." You notice that a large digital display on the wall is showing "94." You see it click to 95, then 96, and finally 97. The receptionist says, "Number 97, please," and a salesperson arrives to assist you. You thought nothing of the numeric ordering of customers, but it's possible that the store had an ulterior motive: they could have been attempting to manipulate the price you would pay. Sound bizarre? Read on . . .

When a consumer views an offer, a key element in the decision to accept or reject it is whether it appears to be a fair deal or not. We know that buying pain—the activation of our brain's pain center when paying for a purchase—increases when the price seems too high. But how does that value equation work? The answer is *anchoring*; typically, we store an anchor price for different products (say, $2 for a cup of coffee for the local coffee shop) that we then use to judge relative value. That sounds simple enough, but it's actually not. Some anchor prices are stickier than others, and at times, totally unrelated factors can affect these anchor points. The better marketers can understand how anchoring works, the more creative and effective pricing strategies they will be able to develop.

Gasoline: Drifting Anchor

First, let's look at a nonsticky anchor price scenario that most of us cope with daily: fluctuating gasoline prices. In the United States, we've seen prices surge past the $4 level, not high by world standards but a new threshold for Americans. The first time I saw that "4" digit at the front of the price, I'm sure my brain registered pain. I had barely become used to paying $3 per gallon of gas. But, after a short time, my anchor was reset. The $4 prices were no longer exceptional, and if I had been seeing mostly $4.29 prices, a $4.09 price would register as a good deal. If I saw a station offering gas for $3.99—a price that only a few months earlier would have seemed outrageously high—I'd be hard pressed not to pull into the station to take advantage of the "bargain." Of course, gasoline is a unique product; we expect its price to vary, and we have constant feedback on current pricing as we pass gas station signs. For this product, we are constantly reanchoring.

Real Estate Prices

Other items have stickier anchor points. In *Predictably Irrational*, Dan Ariely describes research by Uri Simonsohn at Penn and George Loewenstein at Carnegie Mellon University, showing it takes about a year after relocation for home buyers to adapt to the pricing in a new market with higher or lower real estate prices. People who moved and bought a new home immediately tended to spend the same amount on housing as they had before, even if it meant buying a home that was much larger or smaller than the one they left.[5]

Less Familiar Products

But what about items for which we have fuzzier anchors? We get daily feedback on gas prices, and if we own a home, we probably keep an eye on sales of comparable properties to gauge our own level of equity. Items that are unfamiliar or rarely purchased may form an anchor point when we start thinking about the purchase. If we decide to buy a big-screen television, we may spot one we like in a Best Buy circular for $1,000. We may not buy that item, but according to Ariely that now becomes an anchor price against which other deals are measured.

Irrational Anchors

Here's where anchor prices get weird—and *weird* isn't a word I use lightly when I'm talking about the foibles of human brains. Up to this point, there was a perfectly logical framework underpinning the brain's anchoring process. But research conducted by Ariely showed that getting subjects to think of a random number—in this case, the last two digits of their Social Security number—impacted the price they were willing to pay for various items. A higher random number led to higher prices.

Table 5.1 is just one data set from Ariely's experiment—prices that subjects would pay for a cordless keyboard:

Table 5.1   Priming Number Effect on Acceptable Price

Social Security Number Digits	Keyboard Price
00–19	$16.09
20–39	$26.92
40–59	$29.27
60–79	$34.55
80–99	$55.64

For an unfamiliar product like a cordless keyboard, the random number that the subjects were thinking of ended up affecting the price they said they'd pay. The correlation between Social Security number range and price for this data set was an amazing (to me, at least) .52! (Before you start hanging posters with big numbers all over your store, be aware that, as with many of Ariely's clever experiments, this one used subjects who were answering a questionnaire, not actually buying the product.)

Presetting an Anchor

Other experiments by Ariely showed that anchors could be preset for unfamiliar items; in that case, a payment for listening to an annoying sound. A questionnaire that included, "Would you be willing to listen to this sound again for $.10?" elicited lower bids than those given by subjects asked the same question with a price of $.90.

Brainfluence Takeaway: Be Careful Where You Drop Your Anchor!

It's no big news to marketers that customers may have specific price expectations for a product or product category. If one can bring a product into that category with a price lower than expected, it should be an attractive offer. If one's product is premium priced, then it will be important to separate it as much as possible from lower-priced products.

The more interesting challenge is how to deal with new products for which consumers have no clearly established anchor price. Ariely's research shows that anchor pricing for such products is quite fungible, and marketers would do well to avoid inadvertently establishing a low anchor price. If a higher anchor price can be established, then offers involving lower prices will be attractive to consumers.

Apple's iPhone introduction is a good example of using anchor pricing to keep demand strong. When they first released the iPhone, it ranged in price from $499 to $599, establishing the initial anchor for what the unique product should cost. To the chagrin of early adopters, Apple dropped the price by $200 after only a few months, creating an apparent bargain and stimulating more sales. When they introduced the iPhone 3G, pricing was as low as $199, and they sold one million phones in three days.

There are many reasons why marketers start with a high price initially. One big one is to work the demand curve, that is, to demand a high price from the portion of the market willing to pay that much before dropping the price to reach a larger number of customers. A key benefit of this strategy for new products, though, is that a high anchor price is established in the minds of customers, making each subsequent reduction a bigger bargain.

Nonsense Anchors

Can marketers take advantage of irrational anchor pricing? Would asking customers to think of a number between 90 and 99 while standing in line at a fast-food restaurant make them willing to pay more for a burger? Should stores hang posters of big numbers by the checkouts? Although Ariely's work suggests that this kind of irrational anchoring effect could exist, I wouldn't recommend building a marketing strategy around such techniques. But by all means feel free to test it!

Infomercials and Anchor Pricing

One group of marketers that seems to implicitly understand anchor pricing are the creators of successful infomercials. Just about every one of these seeks to establish a high anchor price for their usually unique or unfamiliar product. They start by saying things like, "Department stores charge $200 for this kind of product . . ."; then they make an offer at a lower price. They typically proceed to add bonus products into the offer as well, making the new anchor price of their actual offer ("Only $59.99 plus shipping!") look better and better. By the end of the pitch, the offer price is not only far lower than the initial anchor but the offer itself has expanded to include far more products. (One such commercial, as it concluded, dropped the price by $5 "for callers in the next 20 minutes"—yet another exploitation of a favorable comparison to a previously established anchor.)

Marketers of all types could do worse than studying the techniques of successful direct marketers. The latter live or die by the success of their commercials, catalogs, or websites, and if you see an offer repeated time after time you can be certain that it is working.

6

Wine, Prices, and Expectations

IN AN AREA as subjective as wine tasting, it's easy to believe that what wine drinkers say about a wine is influenced by what they know about the wine. (Or, by what they *think* they know!) It might be surprising to find out, though, that wine thought to be more expensive really *does* taste better at the most fundamental level of perception. Researchers at Stanford University and Caltech demonstrated that people's brains experience more pleasure when they think they are drinking a $45 wine instead of a $5 bottle, even when in reality it's the same cheap stuff![6]

The important aspect of these findings is that people aren't fibbing on a survey; that is, they aren't reporting that a wine tastes better because they know it's more expensive and they don't want to look dumb. Rather, they are actually experiencing a tastier wine.

The price (or what the subjects thought was the price) actually changed their experience with the product. Baba Shiv and his fellow researchers monitored brain activity using fMRI while the subjects tasted the wine to observe how the subjects' brains reacted with each sip.

Wine isn't the only product affected by its price. Shiv, in another experiment, showed that people who paid more for an energy drink actually solved puzzles more quickly than those who bought it at a discount. The higher price made the drink more stimulating.

Yet another study showed that 85 percent of subjects given a placebo pill for pain relief reported a reduction in pain when they were told the pill cost $2.50 per dose; when told the pill cost 10 cents, only 61 percent of subjects reported a pain reduction. The pills, of course, had no actual active ingredients.[7]

Here's the conundrum for marketers: On one hand, we know that the pain of paying kicks in when people perceive that a product is overpriced and makes people less likely to make a purchase. But now we have multiple studies showing that people enjoy a product more when they pay more for it. How should a marketer determine the price point?

I don't think these neural reactions to pricing are necessarily in conflict. If the wine drinkers in the Stanford University–Caltech study had been sent to the supermarket and asked to pick up a bottle of wine on the way to the lab, they would no doubt have felt the pain of paying too much for a bottle of wine. Unless they were wine aficionados, they likely would have chosen a less costly bottle. (Other factors could influence the selection process, too. Would the researchers see the bottle chosen? If it was too cheap, would they think the subject was a wine ignoramus? Would blindly choosing a costly bottle make the subject look like a snob or a spendthrift?) The pleasurable boost from a higher price occurs *after* purchase and consumption, so marketers still face the same problem they always have: setting a price that consumers will accept and that will yield a suitable combination of profit margin and total revenue.

Brainfluence Takeaway: Be Careful With Discounts

What this does suggest is that marketers need to understand that price is an important part of the experience for a premium product or luxury brand. This isn't huge news; we've seen once-proud brands destroyed by overdistribution and pervasive discounting. And it isn't even the price that the consumer pays; the subjects in the study didn't pay anything for the wine they tasted, but they still stated that the expensive wine tasted better.

The consumer has to believe that a product is priced at a certain level for the brain effect to kick in. If someone gives me a $100 bottle of wine, I'll no doubt taste it as such. If I find the same bottle mispriced at the wine shop and buy it for $10, it will likely still be a $100 wine to me (and I'll have greatly reduced my buying pain as well).

But, if I find a bin full of the wine priced at $10 and marked "Huge sale; save $90 per bottle!" some skepticism will kick in. Did this vintage turn out poorly? Did the shop store a few cases next to the furnace and find they had gone bad? Did Robert Parker or another wine expert give it a terrible review? I'm certain that these doubts would lower my brain's perceived value of the wine. If the wine was advertised with a "new low price" of $10, my brain would be even more certain it didn't taste like a $100 bottle of wine.

There's not an easy way to cut through the complex balancing act of pricing the product high enough to appeal but low enough to sell in volume. My advice is to price the product appropriately for the target market and to be aware that discounting may actually reduce the quality of the customer experience. That doesn't mean that discounts or low prices are bad; they have a powerful effect on consumers, too.

Most consumers will have no problem in deciding whether the better taste (real or perceived) of a more costly bottle of wine justifies the difference in price. That's why two-buck chuck has sold hundreds of millions of bottles to date, whereas $100 bottles mostly gather dust on wine store shelves.

7

Be Precise With Prices

IN MY TIME as a catalog marketer, I usually priced products just below the next dollar increment. So, for example, a cheap item might be $9.97 rather than $10, and a more expensive item may have been $499, or even $499.99, instead of $500.

This approach was based on a couple of assumptions. First, I thought that there was probably something desirable about offering, say, a "nine-dollar-and-change" price versus a "ten-dollar" price. Even though the difference was only a few pennies, I thought, some customers would perceive the $9.97 price to offer more substantial savings.

Second, I observed that big marketers like Sears, who could afford to test any number of pricing options and no doubt did so frequently, tended to stick with the "just below the next increment" approach. As it turns out, I was right, but for the wrong reason. New research points us toward the reasons why consumers respond better to a $499 price versus a $500 price, and it has more to do with the apparent precision of the odd number than the lower price.

University of Florida marketing professors Chris Janiszewski and Dan Uy tested how people react to pricing in an auction environment by giving groups of buyers three different starting prices:

- $4,988
- $5,000
- $5,012

While for practical purposes these prices may be essentially identical, when the researchers asked the buyers to estimate the wholesale price of the item, the buyer group with the $5,000 price estimated a much lower number. Not only did the $5,000 group move farther away from the anchor price, but they also tended to estimate the wholesale price as a round number, too.

Janiszewski and Uy attribute this phenomenon to our creation of a mental measuring stick based on the initial price. If we think a toaster priced at $20 is overpriced, we estimate it might be worth $19 or $18. For the same item priced at $19.95, our measuring stick has more precision, so prices like $19.75 or $19.50 come to mind.[8]

Another study looked at the price of houses and found that sellers who listed their house at an odd price, such as $494,500, sold at a price closer to their asking price than houses priced at even numbers, like $500,000. Oddly, the even-priced houses lost more value as they aged on the market, too.[9]

Brainfluence Takeaway: Use Precise Pricing

According to these findings, it seems, I might have done just as well selling a $499 product at $502.50; the key thing is to avoid the dreaded round number of $500, which implies a lack of precision and makes customers wonder if $400 is a more appropriate price.

I still think there might be a small bias toward the slightly lower number than the slightly higher number when it comes to buyer decision making, but the researchers didn't explore that directly. Another area that could use more study is comparing precise pricing to minimalist pricing, such as the tiny "19" (with no currency symbol or decimal) as one might find on a restaurant menu.

This work should give marketers the ammunition they need to fend off requests for simplified pricing. In the past, I recall frequent admonitions that "Nobody is fooled by a price that's a penny cheaper—let's keep it simple and just charge an even number." People may not be fooled by the more precise price, but they may attribute a higher value to the product itself.

8

Decoy Products and Pricing

NEED TO SELL more of a product or service? Here's a counterintuitive idea: offer your customers a similar, but inferior, product or service at about the same price. While it's unlikely that they will actually buy the less attractive item, you may see a jump in sales of what you are trying to sell.

Here's a real-world example. The last time I needed a can of shaving gel, I found myself staring at a shelfful of options. Gels and foamy creams, with variations that included "Sensitive Skin," "Aloe," "Cleansing," and many more, lined the shelves. As I stood there befuddled by the choices, I noticed a taller can of the "Advanced" gel amid the forest of shave products. This can was identical to several other cans of "Advanced," but it was one or two inches taller and held a couple of ounces more of the product. Best of all, it seemed to be the same price as the shorter cans.

I studied the cans for another few seconds to be sure I wasn't missing something. Nope, I wasn't—same stuff, same package design, same price, but 20 percent more product. My confusion evaporated. I had no idea how shaving gel could be "Advanced," or how that might compare with "Aloe," but I grabbed the bigger can, rooted around and found one more in back, and headed for the checkout with both cans. How did buyer befuddlement turn into a larger-than-expected purchase so quickly? The answer: decoy marketing. In this case, the decoy was unintentional, but there are lots of ways that marketers can use the technique to steer customers toward a decision.

In the shaving gel display, the inclusion of the extra large shaving cream can was an accident—the store just had a few left from a previous promotion. But the principle worked just fine. In this case, the regular-sized cans were the decoys. As soon as I spotted a *nearly identical product that was clearly a better value*, that new find stood out as the right choice.

Relativity is the key element in decoy marketing. Our brains aren't good at judging absolute values, but they are always ready to *compare* values and benefits. When used proactively by marketers, a decoy product or offer can make another product look like a better value.

In *Predictably Irrational*, author Dan Ariely describes an experiment using magazine subscription offers. Like most of Ariely's experiments, this one is deceptively simple. Two groups of subjects saw one or the other of these offers to subscribe to *The Economist*[10]:

Offer A

- $59—Internet-only subscription (68 chose)
- $125—Internet and print subscription (32 chose)
- Predicted Revenue—$8,012

Offer B

- $59—Internet-only subscription (16 chose)
- $125—Print-only subscription (0 chose)
- $125—Internet and print subscription (84 chose)
- Predicted Revenue—$11,444

Take a moment to look at this rather startling result. Both offers are the same, with the exception of including the print-only subscription in Offer B.

Despite the fact that not a single person chose that unattractive offer, its impact was dramatic—62 percent more subjects chose the combined print and Internet offer, and predicted revenue jumped 43 percent. The print-only offer was the decoy and served to make the combined offer look like a better value. Although it's true that Ariely's test had the subjects choose without actually consummating the deal with a credit card, it's clear that introducing the decoy made the combined offer look more attractive.

How Decoys Work

According to Ariely, decoys change behavior when a subject is choosing between alternatives that are more or less equally attractive. He gives an example of choosing between a trip to Rome and a trip to Paris, both of which include free breakfasts. One might expect a slow decision-making process with a more or less even split between the two alternatives. Ariely suggests that introducing a decoy, a trip to Rome with no breakfast, would make the original trip to Rome more attractive, and that, given those options, the trip to Rome with breakfast would handily beat the similar Paris trip.

So, jumping back to the shaving gel topic, if a drugstore received a shipment of promotional cans with an extra 20 percent of product inside, their first reaction might be to remove the regular cans from the shelf until the promotional stock was gone. What customer would be dumb enough to buy the small can when the bigger cans were the same price?

According to decoy marketing logic, however, the store would be well advised to leave a few of the small cans on the shelf with the bigger ones. As counterintuitive as it seems, the presence of some small cans would likely boost sales of the larger promotional cans, perhaps even taking market share away from competing products that came in the larger size to begin with.

Decoys in Real Estate

I've bought a number of homes, and I've found that real estate agents often set up a tour of several houses in the same price range, leaving the most desirable for last. This seems to me to be another form of decoy marketing, particularly when the next-to-last house compares poorly with the one the agent hopes to sell you (e.g., the same price but in need of more repairs).

Ariely suggests that this will be most effective when the comparison is between superficially similar homes, for example, between two-story colonial-style homes with the same number of bedrooms. Buying a house is a complex, risky, and expensive process, and getting a buyer to make a decision—even when he or she knows it's necessary—can be difficult. Clever real estate agents learn that comparisons are a key part of the buyer's process and that selecting the right homes to visit is a key part of moving toward a decision.

Brain Scan Evidence

One study used fMRI scanning to see what happens in our brains when we are trying to choose between options. The researchers found that choosing between two equally attractive options caused the subjects to display irritation due to the difficulty of choosing. But, when another less attractive option was offered, the choice process became easier and more pleasurable.[11]

Brainfluence Takeaway: Try a "Not-So-Good" Decoy to Push Your Top Product

I don't advocate any techniques that push customers into buying something they don't need or want. Sometimes, though, customers have difficulty deciding between alternatives. To get the product they need, they require a nudge in one direction or the other. For example, I was certainly going to buy shaving gel in that store, but the unintentional decoy got me to the decision point and on my way more quickly than if I had spent another few minutes considering the weighty issues of gel versus foam, aloe versus sensitive skin, cheaper small size versus expensive big size, and so on. The regular-sized decoys nudged me toward the jumbo can at the same price, and the deal was closed.

When creating their product offerings, most companies try to develop the best and most attractive offers they can—a practice I wholly endorse. But sometimes adding a less attractive offer to the mix will close more deals on the better offers without disadvantaging the customer in any way. So, the next time you are creating your "good, better, and best" packages, consider tossing in a "not-so-good" package that's similar to (but not as good as) the one you'd like to drive the most traffic to. If that boosts sales of that item, you'll know your decoy is working.

9

How About a Compromise?

WHEN MARKETERS PLAN a company's product offerings, they usually try to do so in the most logical way possible. Several levels of product may be offered: a stripped-down, basic version; a more capable better version; and perhaps a "best" version. These are normally priced at quite different levels, probably based in part on the relative manufacturing costs of the products.

In the last chapter, we saw how a seemingly crazy pricing strategy—that is, pricing an inferior product either the same as or almost the same as a better one—could boost sales of the better product. (In that case, the inferior product is the decoy.)

Now, let's look at a different kind of decoy: a new high-end product that, even if it sells poorly, can boost sales of the next product in the lineup.

Retailer Williams-Sonoma at one point offered a $275 bread maker. Later, they added a large capacity version at a 50 percent premium. They didn't sell many of the more expensive model, but sales of the cheaper one doubled.[12]

What happened? Simply put, introducing the higher-priced machine framed the previously most costly unit as a compromise, or middle-of-the-road choice. Buyers were no longer spending too much on the "Cadillac" of the line, but rather making a wise and practical choice. Before the retailer added the higher-priced bread maker, customers may have compromised on a still lower-priced machine, or perhaps bought none at all.

A Stanford University experiment had a group of consumers choose between two cameras, one more full-featured than the other. A second group chose from a selection of three cameras, which had the other two cameras plus one even higher-end model.

The first group split their purchase about 50/50 between the two models. But, in the second group, fewer of the cheapest unit sold while more of the second camera sold. Adding the very expensive model made the second camera look like a reasonable compromise.[13]

Brainfluence Takeaway: Add a High-End Product

From a practical standpoint, this means that if you have a solid product at the top of your line, you can actually *increase its sales* by adding an even higher-priced product above it in the lineup.

You might find, of course, that the market will support the new premium item on its own merits. If that happens, perhaps introducing an even more costly super-premium product might further boost revenue. But, even if the new high-end product doesn't generate spectacular sales, you may find that it boosts sales of the next-best or mid-range products.

Of course, there are a few cautions. First, the customer may not be comparing your products only against each other; keep an eye on competitive offerings, too. Second, you should avoid having too many product variations. Research shows that having too many choices reduces sales, due to a sort of paralysis of analysis.

Restaurant Decoys

One area where decoy products are used with great regularity (and success) is in restaurants. The costly filet mignon and lobster combination at the top of the menu is likely more effective at making the other entrees seem reasonable than in generating orders itself. Similarly, the $100 Cabernet Sauvignon on the wine list makes a $35 bottle an acceptable upgrade compared with the $20 plonk at the bottom of the price range.

10

Cut Choices; Boost Sales

CONSUMERS MUST LIKE lots of choices—why else would there be hundreds of shampoo brands and variants on a typical supermarket shelf? Actually, it's been known for years that *too many choices can reduce consumer purchases*.

A study at Columbia University compared consumer behavior when confronted with a selection of either 6 or 24 gourmet jams in an upscale grocery store. The bigger selection did indeed cause more customers to stop and check it out—60 percent looked versus 40 percent for the limited selection. The interesting part, though, was the purchasing behavior. Whereas 30 percent of the customers presented with the limited selection made a purchase, a mere 3 percent of those who saw the extensive selection bought something.[14]

That result is quite startling—the small selection sold 10 times as much as the larger one.

Choice Fatigue

Additional research shows that making choices tires the chooser's brain and can actually make subsequent decision making more difficult.[15]

One study, by Ned Augenblick and Scott Nicholson of Stanford University, analyzed voting patterns in a California county. They found that the lower on the ballot an item appeared, the more likely the voter was to not make any choice or to use a shortcut, such as picking the first choice. The process of working through the ballot making choices caused voters to look for an easy way out as they progressed.[16]

We've likely all experienced that ourselves when completing online surveys. We start out paying close attention to the questions and choices, but if the process starts to stretch across multiple screens, our diligence wanes.

Cutting choices works in the real world. Walmart dropped two brands of peanut butter and found sales in the category went up. Similarly, Procter & Gamble cut the range of skin care products at a retailer, and sales of the remaining products increased. Customers reported that the product selection seemed larger after the cut, perhaps because the merchandise could be better organized and displayed.[17]

Brainfluence Takeaway: Find Your Choice Sweet Spot

The trick, it seems, is finding the optimal number of choices for your product: offering enough choices to ensure that a customer can find a satisfying product, but not so many that the customer will be bewildered or demotivated. As with most elements of marketing, testing beats guesswork for this kind of decision. If any general conclusion can be drawn, it's that adding more choices because you want to have what looks like a large selection is a bad strategy; if poorly selling choices are axed, sales may actually increase.

Helping Customers Choose

Customer guidance may help, too. In the Columbia study, almost nobody purchased jam products when the selection was huge. What if a salesperson had been on hand to ask customers a question or two about their preferences and then make a strong recommendation? "If you like strawberries, then you'll absolutely love our strawberry ginger jam. It's full of fruit flavor but has really interesting spicy notes, too. A group of chefs rated it their favorite choice from our full range of jams." Likely, a bit of effort to help the customer decide (and validate that decision with additional data) would go a long way toward slicing through the confusion and frustration caused by too many choices.

Self-Service Help

Even in a self-service setting, guidance in the form of labels, shelf talkers, and so on, may help by directing consumer attention toward products that may be suited to their needs and wants. The wine shelves at the supermarket are a good example of a paralyzing array of choices. Wine shops deal with this profusion of options by offering (apparently) expert advice to customers. In contrast, many supermarket wine sections offer as large a selection as a wineshop but have no trained staff to assist confused customers. I've seen smart retailers guide choices by labeling a few wines with prominent descriptions and expert ratings.

Choosing on the Web

Online retailers can offer a greater selection of products than brick-and-mortar stores, and they can use all kinds of techniques to make choosing easier: recommendation engines, sorting and ranking features, ratings and reviews, suggestions of similar products, and so forth. Amazon.com has a product list that numbers in the millions, but it still manages to guide its customers to appropriate choices. Some online retailers fail the test, though. I've left sites that presented me with a large assortment of products that met my initial criteria but offered me no way to sort through them and narrow my options.

Avoid Similar Choices

The wide selection phase of the jam experiment is a good example of offering many choices with no shortcuts to help consumers. Choices are less daunting when the items are quite different and offer the consumer meaningful variation. Sales-killing choices are those that appear very similar and offer the consumer no shortcuts in making a decision.

The basic message is the same for all venues: more choice isn't always good and can actually *reduce* sales.

SECTION

Two

Sensory Brainfluence

THE CONNECTION BETWEEN our senses and our brain is direct. Marketers who build sensory features into their products, services, and marketing can appeal directly to the emotions and stored memories of their customers. Marketing to all five senses can change weak brands and products into powerhouses.

11

Use *All* the Senses

ONE OF THE strongest advocates for creating marketing that appeals to all five of our senses is Martin Lindstrom, author of both *Buyology* and *Brand Sense: Build Powerful Brands Through Touch, Taste, Smell, Sight, and Sound*. The latter book was based in part on a global research project by Millward Brown, which studied the relationship between branding and sensory awareness.

Lindstrom's basic point in *Brand Sense* is simple: brands that appeal to multiple senses will be more successful than brands that focus on only one or two. These appeals can be part of the brand's advertising, like using a distinctive color and logo in a consistent manner, or be part of the product itself, such as a phone ringtone or the fragrance of a soap product.

Singapore Airlines, according to Lindstrom, is the pinnacle of sensory branding. They not only use the consistent visual themes one might expect from an airline but incorporate the same scent, Stefan Floridian Waters, in the perfume worn by flight attendants, in their hot towels, and in other elements of their service. Flight attendants must meet stringent appearance criteria, and they wear fine silk uniforms that match elements of the cabin decor.

Singapore Airlines strives to make every sensory element of their customer interaction appealing and, equally important, consistent from encounter to encounter. Lindstrom credits the firm's perennial position atop travelers' preference rankings to these efforts.

Brand Fragments

One key element of Lindstrom's marketing prescription is what he calls, "Smash Your Brand." In essence, he thinks a brand should be identifiable even when some parts of the marketing program aren't there. If your logo is removed from your product or your advertisement, would it still be instantly recognizable as your brand? Is just a color enough to signify your brand? Of course, few brands have the power to claim a single color as their exclusive look, but the point is that marketers need to think beyond their logo as the sole consistent element in their branding efforts.

Brainfluence Takeaway: Appeal to All Five Senses

To be truly successful, your marketing should encompass every human sense. This isn't an exhaustive list of possible sensory topics, but check them off and see which you are addressing now and which are successful enough that your customers would recognize them on their own:

Sight—logo, product design, color(s), typeface

Sound—music, product sounds

Taste—product taste, edible favors/gifts

Smell—environmental aroma, product aroma

Touch—product surface and shape, marketing materials, environment surfaces

Consistency is the key in building the sensory aspects of your brand. These elements should be the same across time, in any location, and in any use. We'll look at some specific sensory approaches in the ensuing chapters.

12

Does Your Marketing Smell?

MARTIN LINDSTROM, WHOM we met in the previous chapter, thinks smell is particularly potent in bypassing conscious thought and creating associations with memories and emotions. He estimates that 75 percent of our emotions are generated by what we smell, and he is an enthusiastic advocate of incorporating the sense of smell into as many aspects of a firm's marketing as possible.

French author Marcel Proust really did get it right with his concept of "involuntary memory." Proust famously described an avalanche of memories being triggered by the smell of a madeleine, a French cake. He felt that these induced memories were more realistic and powerful than "voluntary" memories which we intentionally try to recall. All the way back in 1935, a study by Donald Laird showed that 80 percent of men and 90 percent of women reported having vivid, emotion-triggering memories evoked by odor.[1]

Scents can affect perception in other ways, too. In one experiment, two pairs of identical Nike shoes were evaluated by consumers: one in a room with a floral scent and one with no scent. Fully 84 percent of the subjects evaluated the sneakers in the scented room as superior.

Marc Gobe, author of *Emotional Branding*, says every brand should have a distinctive smell and thinks that scent is a key success factor in building a deeper emotional bond with the consumer. Gobe cites Thomas Pink, a London-based shirt seller, which scents its stores with line-dried linen fragrance. He thinks that even specific spaces, such as sections of a department store or individual displays, may deserve their own unique scent boost.

Gerald Zaltman, an expert in consumer psychology and author of *How Customers Think,* describes how olfactory and other sensory cues are hardwired into the brain's limbic system. That's the seat of emotion, and by virtue of that connection, smells can stimulate vivid recollections.

Once a scent is embedded in an individual's brain, even visual cues can cause it to be resurrected and even "experienced," according to Zaltman. For example, a television commercial showing a pizza being pulled from an oven can trigger olfactory responses in the brain.

Zaltman sees scents as serving in several ways. They can be memory markers that help a person recall familiar brands more than unfamiliar ones. They can also change the way we process information; a lemon aroma, for example, can make us more alert. Zaltman speculates that scents of that type could be helpful when introducing a new product.

More Scent Effects

Scents can affect behavior and consumer perceptions. One experiment showed that nightclub patrons danced longer when the venue was scented with orange, peppermint, and seawater. When surveyed, the patrons of the scented clubs reported they had a better time and liked the music more.[2]

A test in a casino found that people gambled 45 percent more money in a slot machine when a pleasant scent was introduced into the area. Another test found that changing a shampoo's fragrance but no other performance characteristics caused testers to find that it foamed better, rinsed out more easily, and left their hair glossier.[3]

The fact that a change in fragrance affected customer perceptions of how the shampoo performed in totally unrelated areas is a telling point for marketers and product developers.

Sometimes, we process scents without conscious awareness. In one unique experiment, researchers asked female subjects to smell shirts worn by men who watched either an erotic movie or a neutral one. Virtually all of the women said they didn't smell anything, but the functional magnetic resonance imaging (fMRI) scans of the brains of the women who smelled the shirts worn by the aroused guys lit up in a different way.[4] (This is just one example of why surveys, questionnaires, and similar market research tools can yield unreliable results.)

Bad Smells

All sensory experiences aren't positive. Lindstrom recounts the results of a sensory survey of U.S. McDonald's customers that found that one third of the patrons thought that the restaurants smelled like stale oil. Of McDonald's customers in Britain, 42 percent thought the same, and both groups indicated that this smell diminished their enjoyment of the food. The survey found that other customers liked the smell and that it made their mouths water. It's interesting that although usually bad smells are situational and fleeting—scorched coffee, burned food, and so on—in the case of McDonald's, the consistency of the stale oil smell had reached the point of becoming a brand association.

Brainfluence Takeaway: Own Your Smell

Although one thinks of olfactory marketing as the province of big companies that can afford custom fragrance development, just about every business has smells associated with it. They might be intended or unintended, enticing or unpleasant, but they are there. Getting these under control is key for businesses of every size.

Olfactory Branding

The first, and perhaps most significant, use of scent is for branding. The keys to olfactory branding are consistency and uniqueness. One reason for Singapore Airline's sensory branding success is that they developed a memorable scent and then used it everywhere for years. Regular flyers learned what the airline smelled like; more importantly, they unconsciously associated this scent with the rest of the Singapore Airlines experience: lovely attendants, impeccable service, and so on. A brand's scent need not come out of a spray can or an aroma generator; Barnes & Noble stores have a fairly consistent scent that includes crisp new books and Starbucks coffee. (Then again, perhaps there's a machine in a back room pumping out that smell!)

Hollister and other apparel retailers use environmental scents. Reportedly, Hollister uses its own SoCal fragrance, both spraying it on clothing items and even pumping it outside to attract passersby.

Products

Olfactory product marketing is a bit more straightforward but is still important. In today's supermarkets, is there any doubt that more rotisserie chickens are sold because of the enticing aroma of roasting chicken that wafts around that area of the store? In that same environment, though, there may be many other aroma marketing techniques in use, either intentionally or not. The coffee section likely has a grinder that circulates a coffee aroma as it crushes the beans. Some food stores aren't relying on natural aroma propagation—one Brooklyn grocery recently deployed scent generators to stimulate buying. They introduce scents that are enticing but might be hard to create and maintain by normal means, like chocolate in the candy section and grapefruit in the produce area.[5] Nonfood items can benefit from aromas, too—think linen scents in a bedding store, leather scents in clothing and furniture environments, and so on.

The product itself may use materials like rubber, plastic, wood, leather, oils, and so forth, that carry a scent. These can be enhanced if desired, for impact and consistency. Today, the evocative "new car smell" is at least in part the product of forethought, testing, and even simulated scents.

Retail Environments

In any retail setting, controlling the olfactory environment is important. People will associate smells with the store and products. Do you want to be known for stale oil or something else unpleasant? Don't forget the Nike shoe study in which a pleasant smell entirely unrelated to the product (floral scents and running shoes seem quite disconnected) dramatically increased consumer preference.

Olfactory Dangers

In scents, a little goes a long way. We've probably all had the experience of sitting near an olfactorily challenged septuagenarian who applied a few more shots of perfume than were necessary—and it's not a pleasant experience.

Similarly, a fresh-smelling hotel room is a plus; one that seems to have been doused with gallons of air freshener not only is unpleasant but begs the question, "What are they covering up?" Some individuals are quite sensitive to fragrances and may find strong scents very disturbing. One abortive effort to sell milk by placing cookie-scented ads in bus shelters lasted only a day before city authorities forced their removal. The official reason was the objection of the "environmental illness community."

Scents should be subtle and appropriate to their environment. The smell of fresh-baked chocolate chip cookies would be wonderful in a bakery or coffee shop; in an outdoor bus shelter, the same aroma is rather suspect. Consumers' brains will process that same information differently. In the bakery, that smell is processed as real, but in the bus shelter, it's pegged as artificial. Another location-dependent example is musty books; the smell of old paper, dust, and foxed pages would be quite awful for Barnes & Noble, but might be just the thing to get book collectors and academics salivating at an antiquarian bookstore.

Summary: Think Smell

Smell may be the most potent and direct sensory path to the brain. Check out your products and selling environments, both by direct observation and customer queries. Chances are you have at least one default smell, even if you are doing nothing intentionally aromatic. Determine whether that scent is something to build on or something to eliminate. Consider a branding strategy that includes aroma—that may not be appropriate for every situation, but think outside the box. Follow through into both the product and customer contact environment. What do they smell like now, and can you improve their appeal and/or consistency? Finally, never overdo any kind of scent-based marketing. The customer backlash will outweigh any benefits.

13

Learn From Coffee

COFFEE MAY SHARPEN your thinking, and studying coffee sellers may sharpen your sensory marketing, too. Few firms have devoted as much thought to sensory appeal as purveyors of coffee.

One of the keys to the long-term success of Starbucks has been that its stores offer a consistent and appealing sensory experience. The music, colors, and lighting are all important, but the wonderful coffee aroma is what dominates one's senses on entering a Starbucks outlet.

(Starbucks briefly damaged its own sensory appeal by introducing break-fast sandwiches that smelled like eggs and overpowered the traditional coffee smell. The sandwiches were eliminated until Starbucks found preparation methods that avoided the undesirable aroma.)

Nespresso's Dilemma

I enjoy brewing Starbucks coffee at home, but it never seems quite the same as when I consume it in the actual shop. It turns out that I'm not alone, and that my coffeemaker isn't the entire problem. Yes, coffee in the coffee shop *does* taste better, but not for the reasons you might expect. Research from another coffee provider, Nespresso, shows that 60 percent of the sensory experience of drinking espresso comes from the retail environment![6]

Nespresso, a subsidiary of food giant Nestlé, was faced with a dilemma created by this sensory experience quirk. It had created a home espresso-making system that produced espresso that tasted just like the brew you could find in a coffee shop. Unfortunately, consumers didn't recognize that.

It's not a big shock that home-brewed espresso might not seem as tasty as what you get in a coffee shop. This source bias, along with the improved sensory experience in the shop environment, stacks the deck against home-prepared espresso no matter how good it actually tastes.

To beat these ingrained consumer perceptions, Nestlé first launched upscale coffee shops in major cities for the primary purpose of creating the high-intensity sensory experience people expect, but also with the intention of showing customers they could get the same high-quality espresso at home.

The second thing they did was modify the home espresso-making system to release more aroma. This is a brilliant and, I can testify, often overlooked strategy.

I once owned a Melitta coffeemaker that made superb coffee. In addition to brewing it properly, it stored the product in an insulated stainless steel pot (to avoid flavor degradation from sitting on a heating element). Although the system was not hermetically sealed, the brewed coffee was injected directly into the pot with virtually no exposure to room air. This may be good for preserving the flavor, but you can guess the problem: very little aroma escaped into the environment.

My previous Braun coffeemaker was far less sophisticated, but it could be counted on to fill the house with the enticing aroma of freshly brewing coffee.

Brainfluence Takeaway: Give Your Product a Sensory Tweak

I doubt if many consumer firms have taken as many steps to improve the sensory appeal of their products as Nespresso has. Not only did they modify the product itself to improve the sensory experience, they launched an entirely new channel (their branded coffee shops) just to address the perceived sensory gap in the home environment. Most companies won't want to open up a chain of retail shops, but just about every company could benefit from a sensory review of their key products.

If, like Nespresso, you find that you are missing a sensory opportunity (even though it doesn't relate to the quality or performance of the product), don't be afraid to make changes.

14

Sounds Like Changed Behavior

SOME YEARS AGO, researchers in the United Kingdom decided to evaluate the effects of background music on customer purchasing decisions. They chose a wineshop for this experiment, since wines have identifiable origins, and proceeded to play French and German background music on alternating days. The results were startling: the French and German wines each outsold the other by several multiples on the days the matching music was playing.[7]

These intrepid music explorers also found that enjoyable and appropriate background music could induce customers to accept long waiting times, both on the telephone and in person.

Firms like Muzak built large businesses based on playing subtle music that is barely noticed but that changes the audio environment and, in some cases, changes behavior.

Other research has demonstrated the effects of background music on a variety of behaviors. One study found that children with emotional or behavioral problems learned math more quickly in the presence of calming background music.[8] Another study measured how customer perception of a bank changed when background music was added to the environment. A classical sound track caused a 233 percent jump in bank goer's perception of the bank as "inspiring," compared with their perception when no music was playing.[9]

Brainfluence Takeaway: Find Background Music That Works!

There's no single type of background music that works best in every retail environment. A teen apparel store may find booming hip-hop boosts traffic and sales, whereas a merchant selling organic spa products might choose New Age tracks. As shown by the wine experiment, the products you hope to sell should guide your choice of music.

If you settle for silence, though, or random radio broadcasting, you are likely losing customers and sales.

15

The Sound of Your Brand

MARKETING CAMPAIGNS OFTEN focus primarily on the sense of vision, whether they are purely visual, such as print ads and billboards, or have associated sound, such as television commercials or retail environments. How can marketers go beyond using audio to communicate benefits (or, even worse, speed-read through the legalese of a disclaimer) and incorporate a powerful branding or other marketing message?

Most marketers don't ignore the possibilities of sound when it's an available option. They'll use it productively for mood-setting music or a persuasive voice-over. It's possible, though, to go beyond the obvious.

Muzak has been exploiting the need for background music for decades, although for much of that time, they seemed to be primarily suppliers of bland "elevator music" (relatively neutral instrumentals with extreme frequencies filtered out). This was music designed primarily not to offend. Now, Muzak considers itself an audio branding firm, capable of crafting a musical background particularly suited to a firm's overall branding and positioning strategy.

For example, Muzak crafted a mix of soothing and serene instrumentals to create a spa-like acoustic environment for Joie de Vivre's Hotel Vitale. This was designed to complement the hotel's visual, tactile, and olfactory emphases on natural luxury.

Does audio branding actually work? One has to believe there's a fair amount of guesswork when you are an audio architect trying to create just the right branding music for a firm or environment. Still, it seems likely that a diligent attempt, even if imperfect and difficult to prove effective, is better than ignoring the concept.

The Musical Logo

United Airlines has taken a familiar composition, George Gershwin's *Rhapsody in Blue*, and made it their own (to the dismay of some music lovers). The airline has cleverly used the theme in most of its ads but has modified it in many ways to vary the sound and keep it relevant to the ad content. For example, for a television commercial promoting Asian destinations, the familiar *Rhapsody* theme was arranged in an appropriately Asian style.

Rhapsody appears in airport environments controlled by United Airlines, too. Although nobody wants to sit for hours listening to bastardized Gershwin, it's an interesting addition to passenger transit areas, which are high traffic but where nobody stays very long.

Beyond Music

Music may be a powerful mood setter, but other auditory inputs can have a profound impact as well. We've heard about the Mercedes door-slam team—a group project to get the most appealing sound from a closing car door.

One of the more impressive auditory branding efforts I've seen is from Nextel, the cell phone company that is now part of Sprint. They have always offered a unique walkie-talkie feature that lets fellow Nextel users initiate a conversation instantly by pushing one button. Although most cell features let the user choose from a range of sounds or ringtones, Nextel did something different—something smart: every Nextel phone emits a distinctive chirp when in walkie-talkie mode. This chirp is unique and instantly recognizable by any other Nextel user. They have incorporated the chirp into their TV commercials, and one hears it often in public. This powerful auditory branding message cost Nextel nothing other than the courage to keep the sound consistent across phone styles and generations, and to not let users easily change it. (Unfortunately for the Nextel brand, a variety of business issues have more than offset these branding benefits. In the years since the merger between Nextel and Sprint, use of the Nextel brand has almost vanished in favor of Sprint branding.)

Brainfluence Takeaway: Find and Keep Your Key Audio Branding Elements

Consistent use is the key to effective audio branding. Constant repetition breeds familiarity, whether it is a cell phone chirp or a variation on *Rhapsody in Blue*. Although *Rhapsody* is indeed a distinctive and magical piece of music when performed as Gershwin wrote it, that's not why it has worked for United Airlines. They could have taken any one of many musical themes and, after years of repetition, made that theme instantly identifiable and synonymous with their brand.

Few companies can resist the temptation to swap their theme music and brandable sounds every few years, or with every major new product. I'm not sure why. In contrast, most firms won't change their corporate identity willingly, and often logos last for decades with just minor tweaks. If companies were equally reluctant to change their audio branding elements, far more would have sonic branding that consumers actually recognize.

16

Exploit the Brut Effect

JOHN MEDINA, a developmental molecular biologist and author of *Brain Rules*, describes an amusing, albeit informal, experiment he conducted to evaluate the potency of scent to enhance the formation of memories.[10] Medina ran the test while teaching a complex molecular biology topic to two classes. In one class, before each lesson he sprayed Brut cologne on the wall; the other class received no such treatment. (Medina doesn't relate what comments, if any, students entering the cologne-scented classroom made.) When it was time for the final exam, he sprayed Brut for all students. The students who had received the Brut-scented lectures performed significantly better on the test.

Although this experiment wasn't scientifically rigorous, it is consistent with the theory that memories can be stimulated by sensory inputs similar to those present when the memory was formed. (Think Proust!)

Some marketers are trying this approach in the real world. One South Korean politician sprayed a scent called Great Korea at his campaign events and planned to repeat the process near polling places on election day.[11]

Brainfluence Takeaway: Use Scent to Be Memorable

Although Medina's test was designed to test simple recall, marketers can use this knowledge to help customers make a purchase decision. Stores such as Starbucks and bakeries practice this kind of marketing every day—merely passing by a store lets customers inhale the aroma of coffee or oven-fresh baked goods, no doubt causing a combination of an unconscious Pavlovian response and a recollection of past good experiences in that environment.

What studies like Medina's show, though, is that the scent and memory don't have to be related to be effective; in this case, the Brut smell had nothing to do with molecular biology, but it still enhanced recall of the topic. The consistency of the scent was the key factor in stimulating the memory of the subjects.

(I don't think that repeated exposures to Brut actually makes you smarter, although the design of Medina's experiment doesn't rule out this possibility.)

17

Smelly but Memorable

WOULD YOU PREFER a scented pencil? How about a tennis ball? Tires? You might not care. You might even prefer to avoid the olfactory assault altogether, but research shows you'll remember the product better if it has a scent.

Researchers found that scent enhances a product's distinctiveness. They had subjects evaluate pencils that were unscented, had a common scent (pine), or had an uncommon scent (tea tree). They found that the subjects remembered the scented pencils to a much higher degree than the unscented pencils, and this differential increased over time.[12] In particular, the uncommon tea tree scent produced the most durable memories.

Tagline Recall Enhanced

Of interest to marketers, it wasn't just the pencils themselves the subjects remembered. The product attributes presented to the subjects included claims such as, "Is endorsed with the Green Seal environment standard," "Contains superior graphite lead," and "Are made from premium oak trees that hail from California." The subjects remembered these and other characteristics better for the scented pencils.

Other research helps explain why the unusual scent worked better. Our brains process first-time smells in a different way than familiar ones. The special processing, which can associate the smell with a pleasant or unpleasant experience, is unique to our sense of smell. New sounds, for example, don't form the same kinds of memory.[13]

In reading the pencil study, I wondered about the novelty effect. I might remember a pencil that carried a tea tree aroma simply because such a scent would be unexpected and unfamiliar in the context of a writing instrument. On the plus side, though, the improved recall was achieved without the aid of scent cues. Adding a scent during the testing process would almost certainly have boosted recall even more.

Purchase Triggers

One small but interesting study measured sales of a liquor product in a bar. Patrons who had the aroma of that beverage pumped into the surrounding air while a visual ad could be seen purchased nearly twice as much of the product as those who saw the ad alone.[14]

Brainfluence Takeaway: Unique Scents Boost Memorability

People will remember more about a product, even its ad copy, if it is scented. Since we don't know how effective scent would be if many or all products in a category were scented, it seems likely that there is a first-mover advantage for those who are early adopters of scent marketing. If your product is unexpectedly scented and competitive products are not, people will remember not just the scent but what you tell them about the product.

Another first-mover plus is that, at least in the United States, scents can be trademarked. So, if you attach a particular scent to your product, you can stop competitors from using the same scent.

Although any scent may help, one that is unique will further enhance the memorability of the product and its characteristics. This is borne out both by the pencil study and by research showing first-time scents being stored differently in the brain than familiar ones. If possible, choose unusual scents in preference to common ones.

18

Learn From Yogurt

I'M NOT A big yogurt fan. "Live cultures" would be unacceptable, or even scary, in most foods, but for some reason, they are highly prized in yogurt. Nevertheless, we can all learn something from a neuromarketing study focused on the gooey dairy product.

First, a question: If you were to imagine the process of eating yogurt, starting with seeing the container, picking it up, opening it, inserting the spoon and stirring up the fruit, smelling it, eating the first spoonful, then eating another, which step do you think would be most engaging to your brain?

Dr. A. K. Pradeep, author of *The Buying Brain*, says that most people asked that question choose inserting the spoon and stirring. Certainly, the first creamy spoonful would be a good second guess. When Pradeep's company, NeuroFocus, tested the yogurt consumption process in its labs, however, they reached a surprising conclusion: the key part of the process (as far as the consumer brains they tested are concerned) is grasping and removing the foil covering over the top of the container.[15]

NeuroFocus calls such characteristics neurological iconic signatures (NISs). Another NIS could be the crunch of a potato chip. Pradeep doesn't mention it, but long before neuromarketing, one advertiser found and promoted its NIS: Rice Krispies made the sound its cereal made when combined with milk famous with its "Snap, Crackle, Pop" slogan.

Brainfluence Takeaway: Important Product Characteristics May Not Be Obvious

The finding that pulling off the foil lid was the most significant sensory element in eating yogurt was important to the yogurt-making client that sponsored the work, but it's an important lesson for all product marketers. Don't assume that the obvious product characteristics are the only important ones. With yogurt, one would logically expect taste, texture, and aroma to outweigh mere packaging considerations; in this case, they didn't.

This finding doesn't mean that flavor and other characteristics are not still very important to the success of the product; if the yogurt didn't taste good, or had a funny smell, surely it wouldn't sell.

And although neuromarketing studies can reveal surprises like this, costly research isn't always necessary. The Rice Krispies marketers who decided to let other cereal brands talk about flavor and focus their ads on the sound of their cereal conducted no brain studies, but they turned their brand into a decades-long success story.

SECTION
Three

Brainfluence Branding

Brains Love Brands They Know

Marketers have always understood the power of a brand, but it's only recently that we have positive proof of just how potent brands can be. A study in Germany showed subjects a variety of brand images while their brain activity was being scanned using functional magnetic resonance imaging (fMRI). The images included familiar, well-known brands as well as other lesser-known brands. The results were startling: the strong brands lit up areas of the brain associated with positive emotions, rewards, and self-identification. The weak brands, meanwhile, lit up areas associated with memory (perhaps trying to figure out if they had ever seen it?) and negative emotions.[1]

Brands Trump Senses

The power of strong brands even overpowers our senses. Remember the classic Pepsi Challenge? Pepsi did blind taste tests of their cola versus Coke and consistently came out on top. Pepsi hammered Coke with those results in their ads for so long that they finally goaded the larger firm into developing New Coke. The reformulated Coke was capable of beating Pepsi in blind tests, but it was such a marketing disaster that it almost destroyed the brand.

Read Montague, Director of the Human Neuroimaging Lab at Baylor College of Medicine, repeated the Pepsi Challenge in a new way: he had the subjects taste the products while being scanned by an fMRI machine that let him see how their brains reacted to the colas. In a blind tasting, Montague confirmed the original Pepsi Challenge results. Not only did the subjects say they liked it better, but their brains agreed—one of their brains' reward centers showed five times more activity with Pepsi than with Coke.[2]

When the subjects saw which brand they were drinking, though, nearly all of the subjects said they preferred the Coke. Significantly, the subjects' brain activity changed as well. In the "branded" test, for Coke an area of the brain associated with self-identification lit up to a much higher degree. Even swapping the cola identifications didn't change the results: the Coke brand reigned supreme, regardless of whether the subject was actually tasting Coke or Pepsi.

Given that brands exert exceptionally powerful influences on our brain, let's look at some ways marketers can strengthen their brand and use their brand to good advantage.

19

Neurons That Fire Together . . .

SIGMUND FREUD WAS the first to propose the theory, then Canadian psychologist Donald Hebb refined it, but it took neuroscientist Carla Shatz to compact it into six words[3]:

Neurons that fire together wire together.

Modern neuroscience has confirmed Freud's original speculation by proving that our brains actually change with our experiences, a phenomenon called *neuroplasticity*.

The Monkey's Paw

Researchers have found that training alters brain maps (the locations of the brain that correspond to individual body parts). One experiment attached two fingers of a monkey together for a period of months so that they acted, in essence, as a single finger; tests showed that the previously separate brain mappings for the two fingers had indeed become one. Although this is an extreme example, many other experiments show that training rewires the brain.

Anything for a Smoke

Martin Lindstrom gives evidence of how associations can become hardwired over time in his popular neuromarketing book *Buyology*. Lindstrom notes that tobacco warning labels were found to stimulate craving for tobacco when smokers were observed using fMRI brain scans. The very labels intended to frighten smokers became, after repeated exposure, a cue to smoke. By their presence on every pack of cigarettes, the warning labels became associated with the pleasurable aspect of satisfying a tobacco craving.

I Like It, but Why?

Researchers Melanie Dempsey (Ryerson University) and Andrew A. Mitchell (University of Toronto) set out to test the power of branding messages by conditioning consumers to like or dislike fictitious brand names. They exposed consumers to hundreds of images. Twenty of these images paired a fictitious brand with positive words or images, and another 20 images paired another brand with negative sentiments.

At the end of the process, the subjects were unable to recall which brands had been associated with positive or negative messages, but they *did* express a preference for the positively matched brand. The researchers called this an "I like it, but I don't know why" effect.

To further test the potency of these unconscious brand preferences, Dempsey and Mitchell carried out a second experiment in which they presented subjects with factual product information that contradicted their conditioning. The subjects still preferred the products that they knew to be inferior but for which they had received the positive branding messages.

A subsequent experiment found that even highly motivated subjects were unable to overcome their conditioning. The authors concluded, "Choice decisions of consumers are not only determined by evaluations of rational information (product attributes) but are also driven by forces that are generally outside of rational control."

This series of experiments demonstrates that branding messages can be remarkably powerful, even when the exposure has been brief and the messages (or even brand name) can't be consciously recalled.

Pavlovian Branding

Remember Pavlov, who trained dogs to salivate when they heard the food bell even when no food was present? Brands train your brain the same way. A study at Caltech found that a symbol could become associated with a taste experience to the point where merely showing subjects that symbol caused their brain to light up. The more subjects liked the taste reward, the stronger the learned response was in their brains. Golden arches, anyone?[4]

Brainfluence Takeaway: Keep Your Brand Associations Consistent

The neuromarketing message here is that a consistent experience with your brand or product will *become inseparably connected to it*. Lindstrom found that embedded brand messages like the Coca-Cola and Marlboro red colors, and even red race cars similar to the ones Marlboro sponsored for years could stimulate a desire for the product with *no overt brand or product references*. Although few companies have the scale to market like Marlboro or Coca-Cola, that doesn't mean that the idea of a consistent branding message should be abandoned.

Beyond brand characteristics, customer experience will cause these same kinds of associations. If a customer is consistently pleased by a product or service, that pleasurable experience will become attached to the brand. Conversely, bad experiences will also stick. Once these associations are established, they will be difficult to change.

Your customers' brains are constantly forming new associations. To ensure that your brand is wiring itself the way you want it to, keep your brand experience *consistent* and *excellent!*

20

Who Needs Attention?

A COUPLE OF the key questions we often ask about advertising are, "Did the ad get the customers' attention?" and then, "Did the ad hold their attention?" Although these are excellent and important questions, *a lack of attention does not mean an ad has no impact.*

Attention is a good thing. It makes sense that if we have a viewer's attention and present a compelling ad, we stand a chance of improving the perception of our brand. But what about those times when we don't have the viewer's attention, and the person doesn't even recall seeing the ad?

Low Attention, No Attention

The idea that consumers can be swayed without their conscious knowledge isn't new—subliminal messages were a key premise of Vance Packard's *The Hidden Persuaders* decades ago. There are many contemporary examples of how external stimuli can bypass our conscious mind. The idea of low-involvement processing or low-attention processing gained ground about 10 years ago when Dr. Robert Heath wrote a key article for *Admap*.

Heath summed up the prevailing belief about ad effectiveness[5]:

Traditional theories of how advertising works were based on the hypothesis that it must be processed cognitively by consumers to be effective—in other words, it must capture your attention and interest, and make you "think" about and remember the ad and the message within it. Advertising that does not "cut through" in this way is deemed to be largely wasted.

Heath then proposed that we *do*, in fact, process ads without conscious awareness, that sensory associations are particularly strong, and that when we make a purchase decision, these stored brand associations can indeed influence us.

"Ignored" TV Commercials

Research using television commercials supports Heath's theory. In *Brand Immortality*, authors Hamish Pringle and Peter Field describe a series of experiments conducted by Ipsos that exposed subjects to commercials while they were supposedly reviewing a new TV drama. Afterward, the subjects were tested for recall of the ads and for any change in brand perception. This is a truly massive set of data; the experiments involved 97,000 subjects, 512 commercials, and 47 different companies.

The results showed an average brand shift of 7.3 percent for those subjects who paid attention to the ad and could describe it (high-attention processors). More interestingly, though, even those subjects who paid little or no attention to the ads saw a positive brand shift. Low-attention processors who could recall the ad only when it was described by the researchers saw a 2.7 percent shift, and even ultra-low-attention processors who couldn't recall the ad at all saw a 1.2 percent lift. Not stunning, perhaps, but statistically significant and really not bad for a single unconscious exposure. These numbers look even better when compared with the brand shift in the highly attentive group, a mere 7.3 percent.

Fast-Forward Branding

So if commercials that we don't even recall seeing have an impact, what about commercials we skip over by fast-forwarding past them? Surprisingly, research shows that even these bypassed commercials have an impact. One study by neuromarketing firm Innerscope Research compared subjects who viewed ads normally to viewers who fast-forwarded through the same commercials. As expected, the group who viewed the ads live had the best recall. But, despite the loss of sound and most visual content, the fast-forward group still recalled ads and recognized brands at twice the level expected had they not been exposed to the ad at all.[6]

In *The Branded Mind*, Erik du Plessis devotes an entire chapter to attention and makes a strong case for the effectiveness of fast-forwarded commercials. He backs this up with massive data collected in South Africa over many years of monitoring ad exposures and effectiveness.

One interesting finding reported by du Plessis is that the impact of fast-forwarded commercials is highest when the viewer has seen the whole ad at regular speed at least once. After one regular viewing, apparently there's enough information in the fast-forwarded visuals to stimulate recall; this makes subsequent "skipped" ads nearly as effective as those seen at regular speed.

Branding Without Seeing

It's not commonly known that in addition to our main visual processing system, we have a secondary, more primitive system that feeds directly into our subconscious. The most amazing demonstration of this is the phenomenon of *blindsight*. Studies of individuals blinded by brain damage show how blindsight works. Controlled lab experiments show that some individuals who are truly blind from damage to their visual cortex can navigate around obstacles in a hallway without consciously knowing how they are doing it.

But is blindsight just rudimentary light/dark or outline perception? Surprisingly, the answer is no; "emotional blindsight" exists as well. Some subjects are able to react to images of fearful faces, even though they are not consciously aware of seeing them. From that, we know that this primitive visual system is apparently capable of registering not just objects, but social signals as well.[7]

Since most of your customers don't suffer from rare brain afflictions, is this knowledge of any use? It's impossible to say how this primitive system might process brand imagery, if at all. But, we *do* know that consumers process brand information without being consciously aware of it. There's more than one pathway into the brain for visual information.

Familiarity Breeds Likeability (in Milliseconds!)

Decades ago, psychologist Robert Zajonc demonstrated what is known as the mere exposure effect by showing two groups of non-Chinese-speaking subjects a series of five Chinese ideographs; one group received five exposures to the symbols, and the other group just got one. In all cases, the exposures lasted only five milliseconds or less, too fast for conscious processing. Then, Zajonc showed the subjects a larger group of images that included the original set as well as new ideographs and other symbols. The subjects viewed the images for a full second, more than enough time to be conscious of seeing them. Zajonc then asked how much they liked each one.

The subjects who received five subliminal exposures to an ideograph liked it much better than the subjects who had seen it only once.[8]

The conclusion was that the presence of familiar things, even when we are unaware of the exposure, makes us feel better. Later work has suggested that this effect is related to fluency, the ease with which our brains process things that are more familiar. And although the experiment used ideographs, it's not a big leap to suggest that unconscious exposure to brand symbols might work the same way.

Brainfluence Takeaway: "No Attention" Doesn't Mean "No Results"

In short, reams of data show that even when your ads aren't consciously noticed, your branding message is still having an impact. The key point for marketers is to *keep your brand visible* even when people don't seem to be paying attention.

Positive associations to go with that visibility are better. Do you want your brand remembered in the context of a frustrating wait or a rude associate? Wouldn't a welcoming smile or a pleasing scent be better?

Having said that, the subliminal image research suggests that *any* exposure is better than none and can cause a positive association later. Labeling your products in a way that keeps the brand constantly visible is one approach. Every time the product is used, or carried in public, the brand is exposed. Sponsorships are another. How many people consciously notice who has branded their luggage cart at the airport? Probably very few, but those labels add up to billions of impressions per year.

Samsung is a master of subtle branding via sponsorships. Lately, the firm has been branding airport electrical charging stations. Can you imagine a better way to link an electronics brand with a positive association? Imagine the relief felt by the owner of a smartphone with a dying battery, who, stuck in the airport without a charger, finds this electrical oasis!

You may not have Samsung's marketing budget, but if you control an environment, keep your brand visible. If you sponsor a local event, use brand symbols consistent with the rest of your marketing. Look for creative ways to make many inexpensive brand impressions.

Clothing and promotional items can be inexpensive and provide ongoing brand exposure at no incremental cost. (If you are going to put your label on a promo item, be sure it's something that customers will use or at least keep visible!)

21

Passion for Hire

BRANDS DON'T BUILD themselves. It takes people.

Kate Newlin, author of *Passion Brands: Why Some Brands Are Just Gotta Have, Drive All Night For, and Tell All Your Friends About*, thinks the most desirable brand is what she calls a passion brand. Passion brands are those with which consumers form an emotional attachment and recommend enthusiastically to their friends. Indeed, passionate brands inspire evangelism, and their loyalists are disappointed if friends fail to follow their advice.

Newlin thinks that to create a passion brand, you must hire "passionistas." These employees bring their own passion for the category and the brand. The people they interact with will see their genuine enthusiasm, and some will become infected themselves. Newlin writes, "Passion brands breed passionate followings, very often through impassioned employees. I remember the early stories of Red Bull, when dogged sales guys would bring empty cans to bars and leave them crunched up and strewn around to make it look like the brand was popular, well before it actually was."[9]

In the hiring process, we often focus on the objective facts: education, experience, accomplishments, and so on. If we really want to maintain passion within the group and extend that to customers, we need to be sure we add passion to the subjective requirements.

Tech Passion

For a period of years, I ran an information technology (IT) business and had to hire network engineers and other technical staffers. One of the most telling questions I asked job applicants was, "What kind of computer setup do you have at home?" I tended to hire the ones whose faces lit up as they described complex networks they had built with salvaged hardware and beta-version software. I knew these applicants didn't get into the IT field because they saw a tech school ad promising high salaries; these guys (they *were* mostly guys) reinstalled operating systems for fun! Invariably, these passionate techies were the most up to date on breaking technology news, were the quickest problem solvers, and were respected the most by their customers.

Brainfluence Takeaway: Feel the Passion

Your customers can sense the passion of your people, even if they don't process it consciously. The body language, the speech patterns, and other cues will give your customers the confidence that the person they are dealing with truly believes in your product.

If you want your customers to love your brand, when you are looking at resumes, go beyond the facts and look for passion!

22

Create an Enemy

SOMETIMES THE BEST thing for a brand is an enemy: a rival brand that can be the focus of advertising and customer loathing.

Take Apple, for instance; they are a brand envied by all. The firm that began by building some of the first home computers turned their customers into legions of fanatical evangelists. Indeed, brain scans show that when you put Apple "true believers" in an fMRI machine, their brains light up in the same areas normally triggered by religion.[10]

But, without a Steve Jobs at the helm, or with fewer resources than Apple, is building that kind of loyalty possible? I've got good news: although having a visionary and charismatic chief executive officer (CEO) is a big plus, an iconic leader isn't necessary to build a fan base, or even a fanatic base. One secret of Apple's success lies in an experiment conducted 40 years ago.

The Tajfel Experiment

Psychologist Henri Tajfel wanted to know how seemingly normal people could commit genocide, and he explored how easy or difficult it was to get subjects to identify with one group and discriminate against others. What he found was startling: with the most trivial of distinctions, he could create artificial loyalties to one group, who would then discriminate against those not in that group.[11]

Tajfel tested subjects by having them perform a more or less meaning-less task, like choosing between one of two painters or guessing a number of dots shown on a screen. Then, he assigned each subject to a group, ostensibly based on their answer. When the groups were asked to distrib-ute real rewards, they became loyal to their own group and were stingy with the other group. Many variations on this experiment have been per-formed subsequently, and they have shown that people can develop group loyalty very quickly, even in the absence of real differences. Subjects even became emotionally invested in their meaningless groups, cheering for their own group's rewards and mocking the other group.

Tajfel's experiment led to the theory of *social identity*, which states that people have an inherent tendency to categorize themselves into groups. They then base their identity, at least in part, on their group affiliations, and build boundaries to keep other groups separate.

Us Versus Them

In neuromarketing terms, our brains are hardwired to *want* to be in one or more groups. Brands that can be positioned to put their customers into a group will find that their efforts will be enhanced by their custom-ers' own need to belong. In addition, the brand's customers will likely cultivate a dislike for other brand groups.

Jumping back to Apple, look how they have leveraged an "us versus them" approach for decades. Their "1984" commercial certainly drew a sharp distinction between the lone, attractive, athletic young woman and the lines of brainwashed drones.

A year later, Apple's creepy and somewhat depressing "Lemmings" commercial continued to push people into one of two camps; they again portrayed Windows (PC) users as mindless, in this case as blindfolded businesspeople functioning like suicidal rodents following each other off a cliff. (Lemmings, by the way, aren't actually suicidal; they do engage in mass migration, though, and occasionally enter a body of water that proves too challenging to swim across.)

Fast-forwarding to recent times, we have the wildly popular "I'm a Mac versus I'm a PC" ads. These ads draw a sharp distinction: Do you want to be one of the cool kids, or a dork?

Compare People, Not Products

Note the common characteristic of these and many other Apple commercials: they focus on the *people* who use each product. These ads convey little or no actual product information, and instead mock PC users while portraying Apple users in a favorable way.

Certainly, other brands have successfully exploited this concept, both directly and indirectly. Could the surprising results that showed Coke-branded cola lit up people's brains more than Pepsi (whether or not the beverage tasted was Coke or Pepsi) be a result of more people thinking of themselves as "a Coke person" versus "a Pepsi person"? The famous "Pepsi Generation" campaign was all about establishing Pepsi drinkers as a desirable group (young, attractive, fun), although in the long run, Coke has held its leading position.

Car and truck makers haven't worked the "us versus them" angle very much in their ads, but their owner base has certainly picked up on the theme. Truck owners in particular seem to consider themselves part of groups, as shown by the ongoing animosity between Chevy drivers and Ford drivers.

Our Customers Are Different/Better

Although the "us versus them" strategy works better when products are visible to others (cars, apparel, cigarettes, etc.), there is no reason why it can't be used by any brand that people feel at least a little attached to. It's critical to make your customers feel different and to interact with them in a way that makes that more credible than a passing ad slogan.

The Etsy Approach

Although Etsy, the phenomenal web success story in the arts and crafts market, wouldn't seem to have much in common with a megabrand like Apple, founder Rob Kalin has emulated Steve Jobs in at least one way. Etsy's key "customers" are actually the thousands of artists who choose to sell their wares on Etsy, and Kalin has appealed to this group by positioning himself on their side against big business.

Even as Etsy itself turns into a huge enterprise, Kalin calls himself not CEO but crafter in chief and talks about "the big companies that all us small businesses are teaming up against." This rhetoric seems laughable for a company that has raised tens of millions of dollars in venture capital, but so far it seems to be working. It's us (Etsy and the artists) against them (the suits and big business).

Godin and Tribes

Author Seth Godin echoes this thought, but states it in his own terms[12]:

Brand management is so 1999.

Brand management was top-down, internally focused, political and money-based. It involved an MBA managing the brand, the ads, the shelf space, etc . . . Tribe management is a whole different way of looking at the world . . .

What people really want is the ability to connect to each other, not to companies. So the permission is used to build a tribe, to build people who want to hear from the company because it helps them connect, it helps them find each other, it gives them a story to tell and something to talk about . . .

People form tribes with or without us. The challenge is to work for the tribe and make it something even better.

Brainfluence Takeaway: Make Your Customers Feel Like Members of a Group

Have you been able to make your customers feel different from those of your competition? Does your brand have a tribe? Have you been able to define an enemy group that strengthens the cohesiveness of your own? If you can accomplish this and fan the flames of rivalry, you'll create not only more loyal customers but also brand advocates and evangelists.

Subtle Cues Help

If there is some kind of demographic divide between you and your competition (e.g., your target customer is younger), incorporating even subtle cues can highlight the group distinctions.

A test involving the believability of political falsehoods found that asking undecided voters to write their age on a card nearly doubled the percentage who thought John McCain was senile. Similarly, voters who indicated their race on a card were more than twice as likely to believe that Barack Obama was a socialist.[13]

Undecided subjects gave the "Obama is a socialist" a mere 25 percent probability of being true, a number that jumped to 62 percent when they were asked to record their race.

Let me make it clear that I'm not advocating any brand to make false statements about either their competitors or their own products. This research is, I believe, equally relevant to *true* statements. If you can prime your target audience with cues that separate them from other customer groups that favor your competition, they will be more likely to believe your message.

If you can segment your target customers in a way that separates them from other groups, remind them of that difference, even in a very subtle way. Doing so will amplify the credibility of your message and further their status as a member of your group.

Four

Brainfluence in Print

Who Needs Print?

Many forms of traditional print media are under heavy pressure from digital competition. I've worked with a few firms whose main business had been the printing of paper directories. The advantages of digital media for ease of search and instant updating largely killed the print vehicles, and the firms were forced to develop online directories and other digital media products. Newspapers, magazines, and books are all feeling the heat from digital.

Despite all this, it seems likely that we'll have print media around for many years. In this section, we'll look at how print differs from other media and some specific ways to maximize the effectiveness of print pieces.

Digital Applications

Even though these topics are directed primarily at print use, at least some are relevant to electronic media. Font effects, for example, apply equally well to print and digital.

23

Use Paper for Emotion

DIRECT MAIL IS so last millennium, right? Ultraefficient (and comparatively low-cost) digital marketing seems all but certain to supplant physical paper and ink marketing delivered by actual humans. Hold on, though. It may be a little too soon to shut down the paper mills, according to a study by branding agency Millward Brown. Their research project used functional magnetic resonance imaging (fMRI) brain scans to show that our brains process paper-based and digital marketing in different ways and, in particular, that *paper ads caused more emotional processing.*

According to the study, physical media left a "deeper footprint" on the brain, even after for controlling for the increase in sensory processing for tangible items.[1] From the brain areas activated by the paper ads, the researchers concluded that *physical material (like paper) is more "real" to the brain.* Since it has a physical place, it engages with the brain's spatial memory networks.

The study also found that the tangible materials involved more emotional processing in the subjects. The memories of the paper-based ads were likely to be more vivid and associated with emotions.

A Cautionary Note

Before we get carried away and crank up the printing presses, a few limitations of the findings should be noted. The biggest is that a head-to-head comparison of similar digital and print ads may not represent most real-world marketing situations. Digital ads can do things that print ads can't match, like incorporate video, audio, and interactivity. Furthermore, digital ads can be targeted far more effectively based on user interests (e.g., search terms, adjacent content), past behavior, and other characteristics that print can't match.

Optimizing Paper-Based Marketing

As a longtime direct marketing guy, I'm happy to see that high-tech brain scans show that old-fashioned paper still has some advantages that intangible bits can't match. The Millward Brown study didn't look at how to optimize a print piece, but here are a few quick ideas:

- Think about the *tactile* nature of the piece. Heavier stock and a textured finish could emphasize the tangibility of the mailed item, as could die cuts, torn edges, embossing, and so on.
- Take advantage of the brain's emotional engagement with tangible media and create a message that has an *emotional impact*.
- Build in your *brand imagery*; brand recall may be enhanced by the paper medium.

Digital Lesson

Digital marketers, on the other hand, need to look beyond static banners that are little more than converted print ads. (The ubiquity of the term *banner blindness* is one clue about how ineffective many digital ads are!) I have little doubt that a comparison between a paper ad and a well-targeted, engaging, rich-media ad would at least even things up, if not tilt in the favor of digital.

Digital ads have the potential to stimulate multiple senses, both surprise and interact with the viewer, and overall engage the user's brain. I'm confident that these strengths can offset the tangible advantages of paper in many applications.

Brainfluence Takeaway: Paper Means Emotion

Particularly in the context of a mailing piece that you control all aspects of, or in a glossy magazine surrounded by other upscale ads and content, paper can pack a bigger punch than a similar digital ad. Don't give up on paper, and be sure to take full advantage of paper's benefits.

Digital marketers also need to take full advantage of their medium—simple ads aren't that engaging. Animation, sound, interaction, and precise targeting can boost digital out of the less-engaging-than-paper range.

24

Vivid Print Images Change Memory

REMEMBER THAT FRESH, buttery popcorn you had a few weeks ago? Maybe you didn't really have it at all, and the memory was created by a magazine ad. You might think that impossible, but research shows that some print ads can be impactful enough to create a false memory of having tried a product that doesn't even exist!

Researchers Priyali Rajagopal (Southern Methodist University) and Nicole Montgomery (College of William and Mary) showed subjects either high-imagery or low-imagery versions of print ads for a fictitious popcorn product, Orville Redenbacher Gourmet Fresh, but gave them no product to taste. A third group of subjects was allowed to consume samples of the invented product, which were actually a different Redenbacher popcorn.[2]

A week later, all of the participants were surveyed to determine their attitudes toward the product and how confident they were about their opinions. Amazingly, members of the group that viewed the more vivid ad were as likely to report that they had tried the product as the group that actually consumed the samples. The group that saw the low-imagery ads were less likely to report they had tried the product and had weaker, less favorable opinions about it.

Changing the brand to an unknown name, the fictitious Pop Joy's Gourmet Fresh, reduced the false memory effect. I presume that the more ubiquitous the product and brand, the more likely these false recollections are to occur. Ads for Maseratis and 25-year old Macallan Scotch are unlikely to confuse consumers enough that they believe they drove or drank them.

Brainfluence Takeaway: Use Vivid Images in Print

The real story here isn't that advertisers can create false memories, which seems unlikely in most circumstances. Rather, this study shows the power of print ads that incorporate vivid imagery to leave a lasting impression. Clearly, paper has once again shown itself to be an effective medium. These ads, even though static and two-dimensional, can create the impression of experiencing the product in consumer brains and can increase positive feelings about the product.

The research suggests that it's worth taking the time to create superb images—mouthwatering, well-styled close-ups for food products, for example. For other products, images that emphasize the products' sensual aspects, such as textures and scents, would likely work best, even though the sensory experience will be in the mind of the viewer. Since we experience the world in color, I predict that color ads will beat black-and-white ones for creating the sense of having experienced the product.

These findings are good news for magazine publishers, who can offer excellent quality and realistic reproduction of vivid ads.

25

Paper Outweighs Digital

EARLIER WE SAW that viewing information on paper causes more emotional processing in the brain than viewing the same information on a screen. There's yet another way that paper might be better: its *weight*.

Researchers asked people to study a job candidate by looking at a resume placed on a clipboard. Each subject received either a light clipboard or a heavy one. The people given the heavy clipboards judged the applicants to have a more serious interest in the position than did the group that received the light clipboard.[3]

Weighty Words

As bizarre as this effect sounds, our language echoes it. *Heavy* is a near-synonym for *serious* in some contexts (say, literature or music). The concept of *gravitas* neatly combines both elements. And our print practices reflect it as well. Documents that are designed to impress the recipient are almost always printed on heavier stock and may include features such as a heavy varnish coating that further adds to the perception of weight.

The weight effect could play a role in the paper versus digital question, too. It seems likely that viewing a heavy print document versus reading the same "weightless" text on a screen would show the same effect. If that's true, then the print document would convey more serious impact than the digital version.

Brainfluence Takeaway: Bulk Up for Impact

Until someone actually tests the paper versus digital weight comparison, there are still some neuromarketing takeaways from the clipboard tests:

- A heavier document will create a more serious impression than a lighter one.
- Since tactile sensations so clearly influence our subconscious perceptions, other characteristics of a printed piece, such as rigidity, texture, embossing, die cuts, and so on, can all have an effect.
- If you can't afford a heavy printed piece, have the reader hold a brick while viewing your information. I'm joking, but only because handing a sales prospect a brick might seem a bit strange. The experiments show that even an unrelated tactile sensation can influence behavior, so the brick trick could actually work.

26

Use Simple Fonts

Do YOU NEED to convince a customer to complete an application form? Or, for a nonprofit, do you need volunteers for a charity event? In both cases, you will be more successful if you describe the task in a *simple, easy-to-read typeface*.

Research by Hyunjin Song and Norbert Schwarz shows that the way we perceive information can be affected dramatically by how simple or complex the font is. In particular, their work found that readers of a simple font were more likely to make a commitment.[4]

The researchers expected that getting people to commit to an exercise regimen would depend on how long they thought the workout would take. A longer estimated time would be a bigger commitment, and people would be less likely to sign up. That's all simple logic, but Song and Schwarz decided to test two groups of subjects. The first group saw the exercises described in a simple font (**Arial**), and the second group saw the exact same text presented in a harder-to-read font, *Brush*.

The results were astounding. As shown in Table 26.1, the subjects who read the same instructions in the harder-to-read font estimated that the regimen would take *nearly twice as long*, 15.1 minutes versus 8.2 minutes.

It's no surprise at all that the group who thought the exercise would take only 8 minutes was significantly more likely to commit to the regimen.

Table 26.1 Estimated Time to Complete Exercises Printed in Two Type Fonts

Instructions	Estimated Time to Complete
Tuck your chin into your chest, and then lift your chin up as far as possible. 6–10 repetitions. Lower your left ear toward your left shoulder and then your right ear toward your right shoulder. 6–10 repetitions.	8.2 minutes estimated
Tuck your chin into your chest, and then lift your chin up as far as possible. 6–10 repetitions. *Lower your left ear toward your left shoulder and then your right ear toward your right shoulder. 6–10 repetitions.*	15.1 minutes estimated

Song and Schwarz attribute the difference to cognitive fluency—in essence, how easy it is for us to process and digest information.

They performed a similar experiment involving a sushi recipe. Subjects who saw the instructions in **Arial** estimated that preparation would take 5.6 minutes, while those who read the directions in *Mistral*, a more complicated font, expected it to take 9.3 minutes.

Brainfluence Takeaway: Simple Fonts Spur Action

For years, we've been hearing about KISS: Keep it simple, stupid! It turns out the KISS proponents were right. If you need to convince a customer, client, or donor to perform some kind of task, you should describe that task in a *simple, easy-to-read font*.

Since the perception of lower effort is related to the concept of cognitive fluency, you should also make the type size easy to read and use simpler words and sentence structure. These steps will minimize the perceived effort needed to accomplish the task, and your success rate will increase.

There's no reason why the same approach won't work online, too. Need someone to complete a form? In addition to the obvious step of making the form itself less daunting, be sure your instructions are short and displayed in a simple font.

27

When to Get Complicated

THE LAST CHAPTER suggested that using a simple font is almost always the best approach, but there is at least one situation where fancy, harder-to-read fonts can actually work better than simple ones.

If you are selling a costly product, describing it using a hard-to-read font will suggest to the viewer that more effort went into creating that product. As part of their ongoing cognitive fluency research, Hyunjin Song and Norbert Schwarz of the University of Michigan found that restaurant menus are one such case.[5]

The researchers presented test subjects with a description of a menu item printed in either a simple font or a harder-to-read font. The subjects who saw the difficult font rated the skills needed by the chef significantly higher than the subjects who saw the simple font.

Hence, a restaurant wanting to justify higher prices should print the menu descriptions in a more complex font. Other steps that affect the cognitive fluency characteristics of the description could amplify the effect of the fancy font. Long descriptions with big words will also slow down the reader and imply that more effort and skill go into preparing the dish.

Of course, it is logical that the actual copy should also describe, or at least suggest, the skill and time needed to prepare the dish. As with most marketing efforts, best results occur when all the elements are coordinated.

Brainfluence Takeaway: Use Complex Fonts and Big Words to Enhance Your Product

There's a lesson here for all kinds of businesses: complicated fonts and difficult text make things seem harder. If you want to convince customers that your product involves tedious steps to make or that great skill is required to deliver the service you provide, slow the reader down with a harder-to-read font and big words.

Complexify With Caution

One danger in trying to exploit cognitive fluency using fancy fonts and complicated text is that the reader may attach the complexity to the wrong product attribute. So, you might have spent thousands of programming and testing hours making your software exceptionally user-friendly, but if you go into a long, fancy-font description of that effort, the customer takeaway may be "hard to use."

The other danger is that your potential customers won't be motivated enough to struggle through hard-to-read text. Restaurant customers are likely to read the descriptions because they have no choice if they want to order food and know what they will get. On the other hand, customers looking at a product brochure or a print ad might simply skip the text altogether. Could a lingering sense of complexity still remain, even from a brief glance? Perhaps, but I'd recommend using this approach sparingly; overdo it and you might lose the customer's attention completely.

28

Memorable Complexity

IF YOU WANT someone to remember your information, should you use a simple, easy-to-read font or one that is more complicated and difficult to read? Most people would guess that simplicity is best. Surprisingly, though, those who opted for simplicity would be wrong.

A Princeton study compared student retention of course material presented in both simple fonts and more complex fonts and found that retention was significantly better for the complex font.[6]

Why is this? It appears that the additional effort required to read the complex fonts (also called disfluent fonts) leads to deeper processing, and ultimately better recall. The simple font tested was **Arial**; the complicated ones were **Comic Sans Italic**, *Monotype Corsiva*, and **Haettenschweiler**.

This study was conducted with the idea of enhancing recall in education environments, but the same concept has marketing applications. If you want a reader to remember something—a phone number, for example, or the key advantage of your product versus its competition—making the reader's brain work a little harder to read it can produce a more persistent memory.

I don't think I'd start setting long paragraphs of ad copy in Monotype Corsiva just yet, though. We know that people associate much greater effort with disfluent fonts, and seeing a dense block of text in a hard-to-read font might dissuade the viewer from even attempting to read it.

Or the reader might start the text but give up sooner than if it had been in a simpler font.

Brainfluence Takeaway: Boost Recall With Complex Fonts

Use a difficult font to boost recall of important marketing information. But, don't overdo it; use it for a tagline or a phone number, but not for lengthy ad copy. Too much complexity, and your brilliant copy won't get read at all!

SECTION
Five

Picture Brainfluence

HUMANS ARE READILY able to interpret pictures as representations of reality, and that makes photos and illustrations powerful accompaniments to other advertising content.

29

Just Add Babies!

SINCE THE EARLY days of advertising, it's been axiomatic that pictures of babies grab the attention of readers more effectively than any other kind of image. This has led advertisers to stick baby pictures in ads for every kind of product or service, whether or not infants are remotely relevant. As it turns out, all those advertisers were right on the money: our brains are wired to respond to baby faces, and even baby-like characteristics in adults.[1]

How we react to baby pictures was the topic of study using a neuroimaging technique called magnetoencephalography (MEG), which allows extremely fast measurements of brain activity. Amazingly, in as little as 150 milliseconds after being shown a photo of a baby's face, a high level of activity was observed in the viewers' medial orbitofrontal cortex. This area of the brain is associated with emotion. Adult photos had little or no effect on the same area.

There's probably a good evolutionary reason for this. Human babies are vulnerable creatures, and their chances for survival are greater if they tug at the emotions of not just their parents but also of other adults.

The appeal of baby photos is a prime example of how neuroscience research will often serve to confirm what marketers have known either intuitively or through traditional research techniques. An intriguing aspect of the research is that the baby programming in our brains also affects how we perceive adult faces. Studies show that men prefer female faces with baby-like features. Women's preferences are more complex, and depending on their stage of ovulation, may prefer faces that are either more masculine or more baby-like.

Brainfluence Takeaway: Baby Pictures Draw the Eye

If you want to get viewers' attention, show them a baby picture. Of course, you then have to channel that attention into your product or your brand message, which might be difficult if babies are totally irrelevant. Still, we knew babies were attention getters before brain scans, and now we have a better understanding of how and why they have that effect.

30

Focus, Baby!

IN THE PREVIOUS chapter, we saw that baby pictures are a powerful way to attract readers and engage their brains. Now, let's look at a technique proved to increase the attention paid to not just the cute baby, but also your message!

Employing eye-tracking technology to measure the direction and duration of his subjects' eye movements, Australian usability specialist James Breeze studied how people view ads with babies.[2] When the subjects viewed an ad with the baby looking straight out of the page, the heat map shows that viewers fixated on the baby's face and gave quite a bit less attention to the headline and ad copy. That the baby's face would dominate the user's attention is no surprise.

But then Breeze tested an alternative ad version with a side-facing baby image in which the baby is looking toward the ad's headline. In this version, the baby's face was still a major hot spot, but the *ad headline and copy get far more attention!*

Breeze concludes, "In advertising we will look at what the person we see in an ad is looking at. If they are looking out at us we will simply look back at them and not really anywhere else."

Brainfluence Takeaway: Use the Baby's Gaze to Direct Attention

A face in your ad will attract attention, but be sure the face is looking at what you want the viewer to see—your headline, a product image, or whatever is key. Viewers will examine the face, and then subconsciously be drawn to what the eyes appear to be looking at. Try it with pictures of adults, too. Instead of a smiling model staring out of the page, position him so that he is looking at your most important content!

31

Pretty Woman

FIRST, A QUICK question for our male readers: How many additional points of interest on a loan would you pay if the loan offer included a small picture of an attractive woman? I'm sure all of you guys are saying, "For a little picture? Not a penny more!" As with many attempts to predict our own behavior, you'd be wrong.

Marketers are constantly facing the challenge of how to make an offer more attractive to their customers. Will free shipping garner more orders than a $10 coupon? What about a 10 percent discount or a free tote bag? Smart marketers know there is only one way to definitively answer this kind of question: test the options in the marketplace.

One South African bank trying to boost its loan business did just that. They mailed 50,000 customers a loan offer and used several variations in the direct mail package. First, the offers included a range of randomly selected interest rates. Logically, the interest rate (along with repayment terms) is by far the most important factor in whether a loan offer is appealing. In essence, the interest rate is the price of the loan.[3]

With some of the offers, the bank also included several psychological features—details of the mailed offer that had nothing to do with the loan itself but were intended to frame the offer in some way or otherwise alter customer behavior. The researchers were surprised that these irrelevant offer changes didn't just boost the response of some offers, but actually offset the impact of significantly higher interest rates on loan sign-ups.

The experiment featured a rather dramatic range in interest rates—3.25 percent to 11.75 percent. They also incorporated different features in the offer, including different descriptions of the loan, a comparison to competitive products, varied photos of males and females, and subtle suggestions.

Although the interest rate was indeed important, some of the psychological features also significantly affected conversion. Oddly, the psychological features offered the biggest benefit to the less attractive offers.

The education levels and income of the customers did not affect the performance of the psychological features. The researchers concluded, "Even in a market setting with large stakes and experienced customers, subtle psychological features appear to be powerful drivers of behavior."

For me, at least, the most startling finding was that for male customers, including a photo of a female instead of a male on the mailing piece increased response rate by the same amount as a 4.5 percent drop in the loan interest rate. Female customers, meanwhile, were mostly unaffected by the gender of the photo.

I find it amazing that the effect of a mere photo of a woman on a loan offer was equivalent to nearly a 5 percent difference in the loan interest rate—an enormous differential in the lending world.

Brainfluence Takeaway: Test People Photos

Will slapping a photo of a pretty woman on your direct mail piece boost response rates? If you are marketing to men, maybe. Women seem to be much less affected by irrelevant photos, according to this test. That might be good news—women shouldn't be negatively affected if a female photo is used in an attempt to boost male response.

The second takeaway from this research is that marketers should never assume they know what is going to work; testing different offers, different presentations, and even a crazy idea or two is the *only* way to know what will really make an offer take off.

32

Itsy, Bitsy, Teeny, Weeny . . .

IF A PICTURE of an attractive woman is worth four or five points of interest on a loan, what if she was clad in a bikini?

Scantily clad women have been used to sell products to men for decades, and likely for millennia in one form or another. There's little doubt that the typical male brain is wired to respond to attractive females in revealing attire. But is this a cheap attention-getting trick that has no real impact on sales, or does it actually work? Researchers shed new light on this topic by exposing subjects to either videos of women in bikinis or more neutral videos, and then evaluating their decision-making ability.

The researchers found that guys studying bikini-clad girls make worse decisions when presented with a monetary offer. Specifically, the male subjects were offered the choice of a sum of money immediately (about $25) or the ability to negotiate for a bigger amount a week or a month later. In each test, the men who viewed the sexier images chose delayed reward amounts lower than the other men. For example, the bikini watchers might demand just $7 for waiting a month, while the control group held out for twice that.

Although there were individual variations, and not every man was affected similarly, the averages consistently showed that men primed by the sexy video were willing to strike a quicker, less beneficial deal. The researchers thought that viewing the sexier images made the men more impulsive and interested in immediate gratification.[4]

More Arousal, Worse Decisions

An earlier study by neuroeconomics expert George Loewenstein of Carnegie Mellon University and Dan Ariely of MIT surveyed young men who were not sexually aroused and then repeated the same questions when they were. The aroused males gave very different answers about topics like having unprotected sex or getting their partner drunk to make her more pliable. As in the bikini study, being sexually aroused caused the male subjects to be more focused on short-term gratification than on long-term logic. In the words of writer Brian Alexander[5]:

> In general, though, all our brains, Loewenstein believes, can be thought of as being of "two minds," there is the affective system, ("Dude! Who cares what it costs! She's hot!") which answers to our basic drives, and the deliberative system ("That's your IRA contribution!"). To think of this another way, picture an angel on one shoulder and the devil on the other. Even in the heat of the moment, there is still that little voice that says "You know you are making a mistake"—the trouble is it gets drowned out by the volume of the affective system.
>
> We are constantly negotiating between these two systems, which is why economists are so interested; it's how we make purchasing decisions.

Bigger Is Better, and It's Not What You Are Thinking!

When using a photo of a woman to attract the attention of a male audience, what should you make bigger? You may think you know the answer to this . . . and if you guessed her pupils, you would be right! Researchers asked men to rate 8″ × 10″ photos of women for attractiveness and used photos in which half the women had dilated pupils, an indicator of arousal, and half didn't. Although the men weren't consciously aware of this difference, they rated the women with dilated pupils as more attractive.[6]

Brainfluence Takeaway: Sexy Women Affect Male Decisions

What does this mean for marketers? Were the toolmakers who sent out pinup calendars on the right track all along? Do women in bikinis really sell? The answer is, "Probably, and under the right conditions."

To begin with, this effect seems to be a short-term one that would be most effective at the point of purchase. The ideal selling situation, no doubt, would be to have the bikini-clad babe selling to the guys in person. That would ensure both maximum impact and the ability to direct the purchasing behavior to the desired product.

Most products aren't conducive to such a sales approach, though, and a somewhat effective alternative might be posters, point-of-purchase displays, and even product packaging. Marketers, of course, should be aware that female buyers might find the same images off-putting. In addition, marketers should ensure that the images are consistent with the brand image. It would make no sense to cheapen a brand's perception for a fleeting sex appeal boost.

Something that marketers need to watch out for, though, is the reverse neuromarketing effect of sexy advertising. Other research shows that sexual images and situations can actually reduce brand recall. (That research compared recall of ads running on sexy television shows with those on tamer fare.)

In short, for products where bikini-clad babes represent an appropriate marketing strategy (I'll let you be the judge of what those product categories are!), the place to put them is at the point of sale. I'd use them in ads more distant from the point of purchase, like television commercials or print ads, only if they are an integral and long-running element of the brand strategy.

As a more subtle strategy for ads that you hope will appeal to men, be sure the model's eyes are visible and her pupils are dilated.

33

Photos Increase Empathy

WE KNOW PICTURES get our attention, but an interesting experiment showed that radiologists are more meticulous when a photograph accompanied a patient's file. The doctors also said they felt more connected to the patients; radiologists rarely see patients face-to-face.[7]

So, the mere inclusion of a patient photo altered the behavior of these medical professionals, without them realizing that they were treating the patients differently. This might have implications for how medical records are kept and transmitted, but how can marketers use this knowledge?

Brainfluence Takeaway: Include a Photo If Empathy Will Help Your Cause

Nonprofit Marketers

Most organizations looking for donations already understand the power of personal photos. Savvy nonprofit marketers include photos, names, and often detailed biographies of the recipients of their charity. Rather than exhorting donors to "wipe out hunger" in general terms, a mailer may show a photo of a child made even more specific by including her name and specific circumstances. Colleges soliciting donations take a similar approach by including the photos and stories of individual students who benefit from the funds.

Photo Business Cards?

Except in real estate and a few other fields, photo business cards and letterheads aren't common—and might even seem a bit unprofessional. You certainly wouldn't expect to find the business card of a Fortune 500 CEO emblazoned with a grinning photo.

Nevertheless, marketers might well want to look for ways to build photos into their efforts. Not random stock photos, of course, but photos of the individuals in actual contact with the customer. For example, if a company routinely sent out prospecting letters to schedule sales appointments, they could include a photo of the salesperson on the letter. When she calls to schedule an appointment, that small effort will result in a little extra attention.

The evidence that photos of people *do* alter behavior is mounting. The challenge for marketers is to determine what works in their particular situation.

SECTION

Six

Loyalty and Trust Brainfluence

LOYALTY AND TRUST are usually associated with human-to-human relationships, but they are equally applicable to brands. Loyalty is an amazingly potent tool when it can be established in that it reduces marketing expense—retaining a loyal customer is far cheaper than trying to convert new buyers. Even more important, a truly loyal customer can turn into a strong brand advocate and further extend your marketing reach.

34

Build Loyalty Like George Bailey

REMEMBER GEORGE BAILEY? In the movie *It's a Wonderful Life*, he's the fictional businessman who shifts from despair to intense motivation when an angel intervenes to show him how much worse off his town would have been without him. Most of us don't have a guardian angel named Clarence to show us alternative histories, but imagining what-if scenarios is a powerful tool in real life.

Instant Loyalty, Just Add Imagination

Loyalty is an important commodity. Businesses want loyal employees. Marketers want loyal customers. Generally, loyalty is earned over time, but it turns out that feelings of loyalty can be increased in a rather simple way. Researchers at Northwestern University and the University of California, Berkeley, led by Hal Ersner-Hershfield found that having subjects visualize historical alternatives made them more patriotic. Similarly, reflecting on the shaky origins of a company made its employees more positive about the firm.[1,2]

The researchers ran a series of tests. They asked subjects to reflect on how the United States came into being. Half of the subjects were asked to reflect on what their world would be like if the country hadn't come into being. (This is called counterfactual reflection.) The other half were told to think about what their world is like because the country *did* come into existence (factual reflection). The subjects told to imagine the "what if the country hadn't come into existence" scenario demonstrated higher levels of patriotism in subsequent testing than those who reflected on their actual situation.

And it's not just patriotism that can be stirred by imagining alternative scenarios—it works for businesses, too. A similar test that had subjects reflect on the origins of a company showed a significant boost in positive feelings among those who thought about the counterfactual condition, that is, the differences in the world or their own lives had the company *not* been created.

Brainfluence Takeaway: Use Counterfactual Scenarios to Boost Loyalty

What if the company hadn't survived? Most companies have had some touch-and-go moments in their history. The authors of the study cite FedEx as a famous example. The company was almost out of cash when founder Fred Smith flew to a Las Vegas casino in a last-ditch attempt to generate enough funds to make payroll. (Yes, he won enough hands of blackjack to pay his employees. Today, the firm employs 275,000 people worldwide, and it's doubtful that any casino has limits high enough to make *that* payroll!) Just about every company has some sort of story like that (although perhaps not quite as dramatic), and letting employees think about how their situation would have been affected had things not turned out as they did could boost feelings of loyalty.

What if you hadn't joined our company? The researchers didn't test this approach, but I think it likely that, particularly for employees who have had positive experiences since being employed, such as promotions, pay increases, home or car purchases, and so on, reflecting on the company's role in this and, more important, the alternative scenarios, could amplify positive emotion toward the company.

What if you didn't buy our product/service? Has a customer had a positive experience or received real benefits from the relationship? Has the customer reduced his or her cost or improved his or her efficiency?

Have there been fewer delivery problems than with past vendors? Helping customers visualize alternative scenarios would be one way to enhance their positive feelings about the relationship.

Use with caution. There are a lot of ways a poorly planned approach to this technique could backfire. If you call an employee into your office and tell him, "Think about what your life would be like if you weren't employed by us," the emotions generated likely won't be positive. Similarly, telling a customer, "Imagine how screwed up your manufacturing schedule would be if you were still dealing with your old, unreliable supplier," won't come across as positive and professional.

But, if you avoid the ham-fisted approach and are subtle in introducing alternative scenarios, you will produce the desired positive boost in loyalty and emotion without alienating the other person. Of course, if you *can* hire an angel named Clarence, do it!

35

Reward Loyalty

IT SEEMS LIKE everyone has a loyalty program these days. Buy a cup of coffee, and you get a punch card that promises a free cup after you purchase a specified number of additional cups. Shop at the grocery store, and you get points to reduce the price of gas. Our wallets bulge with partially punched cards, and our key rings are stuffed with plastic bar code tags, all in the name of loyalty. Do these actually work?

The short answer is "yes." Researchers in Singapore found that consumers were indeed motivated by loyalty programs. They used credit cards, which they considered an ideal test because credit cards tend to be similar in characteristics and are easy to switch if a customer carries several at once. Credit cards with attractive reward programs were indeed more effective in gaining a larger "share of wallet." That is, people used those cards whose rewards programs they preferred more often than they used other cards.[3]

Obviously, for a loyalty program to work, several factors must be considered:

- The underlying product or service must be at least comparable to the competition in the eyes of the consumer.
- The rewards offered must be attractive to the consumer.
- Brand preferences and other factors may trump loyalty programs.
- "Switching costs" (sacrifices that consumers must make in order to change brands) may increase loyalty to the current brand and reduce the impact of competing loyalty programs.
- Purchase frequency must be high enough to keep customers engaged in the program. Coffee and gasoline, for example, are perfect; appliances and autos are not.

Loyalty Point Power

Providing more evidence of the potential of loyalty programs, one study showed that irrelevant information (in this case, largely valueless loyalty points) changed consumer buying decisions.[4]

What the researchers identified in their experiments went beyond the logical and expected effect of a loyalty program: the *mere presence of point values* influenced customer buying decisions. Even when the value of loyalty points was less than the value of a real-money price difference, the consumers were swayed by the loyalty points.

Starbucks Versus Panera

Electronic programs are ideal, because they allow customer buying behavior to be tracked and make it easy to apply special offers or bonuses. Two current examples are both from the coffee shop genre. Starbucks combines their loyalty program with their reloadable gift cards. Paying with the gift card updates the loyalty program, and the customer needs have only one card. Starbucks further builds on this by issuing customers a special gold card after a set number of purchases. The gold card has some tangible benefits, like free coffee refills, but also confers a higher status on its holder.

Another coffee purveyor, Panera Bread, doesn't combine its money cards and loyalty, but it stores bonuses within the loyalty program. A customer may be awarded a free pastry, for example, and is notified by the barista when the card is used. (Oddly, Starbucks sends its reward notifications, like a free cup of coffee, by old-fashioned snail mail. Perhaps they determined that an actual postcard has greater impact than an invisible electronic update?)

Neither Starbucks nor Panera uses any kind of point system readily visible to the customer, nor does either create the illusion of progress. The old-fashioned punch card beats both programs in that respect. Both programs do provide extra rewards early on to engage their new plan members.

Brainfluence Takeaway: Offer Loyalty Rewards

Assuming your product or service is purchased frequently enough, offer your customers a loyalty program. They *do* work. In addition, keep your customers engaged by letting them monitor their progress and, if possible, reminding them about the program if they haven't bought in a while.

Beyond the loyalty effect, merely exposing customers to point values at the time of purchase can amplify the effectiveness of the loyalty program. Want to encourage sampling of a new product or drive upgrades? Want a customer to visit you instead of your competitor? Try something along the lines of, "100 extra Rewards Points with every purchase!" Note that bigger numbers may seem more important to consumers, so a little point inflation could be a good thing.

Mobile

There's little doubt that mobile marketing technology and personal targeting will create even more effective loyalty programs. (And, perhaps, that annoying pile of plastic loyalty cards will be a thing of the past!) If you have a loyalty program, or are planning one, be sure to evaluate how it will function with mobile targeting.

36

Loyalty, Rats, and Your Customers

So WHAT DO rats have to do with loyalty programs? Well, back in the 1930s, researchers made an interesting discovery: rats running a maze to reach food ran faster as they got closer to the food. This finding led to the goal gradient hypothesis, which states that the tendency to approach a goal increases with proximity to the goal. Simply put, the closer the goal, the more effort you expend to get there.

A few years ago, Columbia University researchers examined the goal gradient hypothesis using unwitting human subjects instead of lab rats, and they found that people pursue rewards much as rodents do. Give people a coffee punch card that rewards them with a free coffee when it's full, and like the rats in the home stretch of the maze, they'll drink coffee more frequently as they approach a fully stamped card.

Similarly, users rating songs online in return for reward certificates visit the rating site more often, rate more songs, and stay longer as they get closer to earning a reward.

One of the most interesting findings was that the mere *illusion of progress* caused people to buy coffee more frequently. The experimenters issued two different cards: empty cards with 10 spots to stamp and cards with 12 blanks of which two were prestamped. In both cases, 10 stamps were required to earn the free coffee. Despite the identical number of stamps needed, the group that started with apparent progress on their card bought coffee more frequently than the empty-card group.[5]

Brainfluence Takeaway: Give a Head Start

We know loyalty programs work. But, rather than just giving people a card (or online account), give them a head start on their first goal. Since we perceive progress as a percentage of completion, providing someone with the goal partially achieved can be an effective boost to a loyalty program. A plane ticket that requires using 25,000 frequent flyer miles would not seem as "close" as one that requires 35,000 miles but in which the customer starts with 10,000 miles. Coffee shops should add a cup or two to the requirement for a free coffee, but then have their staff give an equivalent number of bonus punches upon first use. Not only will the card seem closer to completion, but the establishment and personnel will score points for being generous.

Although loyalty programs may not be right for every product, when they are appropriate, it's clear that quickly moving people toward a reward goal will keep them motivated and loyal.

37

Time Builds Trust and Loyalty

TODAY MORE THAN ever, it seems, there is a huge emphasis on productivity in sales and customer service. Increasingly, businesses give customers tools to place their own orders, check on their status, and so on. In-person sales calls cost hundreds of dollars (some estimates run over a thousand dollars, and trips to distant places cost even more), so an emphasis on efficiency is understandable. And, as a customer myself, I appreciate being able to initiate orders, check on them, and so forth, at any time of the day or night.

Customer relationship management (CRM) software further strives to improve the productivity of sales contacts by helping separate customers into priority groups, with the most important getting the most contact. A key benefit of CRM systems is that time "wasted" on less valuable accounts can be minimized.

In this drive for efficiency, though, companies need to be aware of the importance of contact time to the customer relationship. Let's look at three wildly different groups of "customers" and see how contact time played an important role in their satisfaction.

Convicted Felons

How do you think that felons—convicted felons, that is—would rate the fairness of their legal process? One might expect a rather high level of dissatisfaction (their defense was unsuccessful, after all), with the main variables being objective measures such as length of sentence. In fact, according to authors Ori and Rom Brafman, when researchers surveyed hundreds of such felons, length of sentence *was* a major predictor of their fairness rating. Short sentences made the legal process fairer; longer sentences, less so.

The surprising finding was that nearly as important as the outcome was the time their lawyer spent with them. The felons who had more face time with their lawyers considered the process fairer than other felons with the same outcome. The Brafmans note that "although the outcome might be exactly the same, when we don't get to voice our concerns, we perceive the overall fairness of the experience quite differently."[6]

Venture Capitalists

Despite the rapacious behavior ascribed to them by entrepreneurs, one would have to admit that Silicon Valley venture capitalists are quite a bit different from the drug dealers and armed robbers in the felon study. But it turns out that the venture capitalists and felons have more in common than a desire for high returns on invested time and money.

When surveyed about their investments and relationships with the management teams at those firms, the researchers expected a hard-headed focus on the monetary return of each investment. After all, the objective of the activity is to earn a high return on capital, and venture capitalist firms sink or swim based on their numbers.

Surprisingly, according to the Brafman brothers, the researchers found that the amount and timeliness of feedback from the entrepreneurs was a key factor in the level of trust extended by the venture capitalists and their level of support for management strategies. The Brafmans note that the willingness of an entrepreneur to keep investors updated has little to do with the bottom line and could sway the venture capitalists into less-than-optimal decisions. (It's possible there is a correlation between how good or bad the situation is at the firm and the willingness of the entrepreneur to talk to the venture capitalists, making this bias not entirely irrational. The researchers attempted to control for this in their analysis.)

Injured Patients

In *Blink*, Malcolm Gladwell notes that most people who suffer an injury due to doctor negligence don't sue. Based on extensive interviews of injured patients, it turns out that patients who sue have often felt like they were rushed, ignored, or otherwise treated poorly by their physician.[7]

Think about that. Most people who have suffered a potentially devastating injury because of a medical error do *not* sue their doctor if they feel that they were treated fairly and that the doctor was doing his or her best. This belief, in turn, is based on the quantity of time spent and the quality of that interaction.

Brainfluence Takeaway: Quality Contact Time Counts

These diverse data points show that all customer relationships need to include time spent listening to the customer. This may mean face time for big customers, perhaps phone time or web chat for smaller ones. And these contacts can't be one-way sales pitches—the customer needs to believe his or her concerns are being heard.

Is this difficult? Often, yes. Is it expensive? Perhaps not. Just about every customer relationship is tested at some point—missed delivery dates, unexpected price increases, or an aggressive competitor. If you want your company to be like the doctors whose patients defends them, even after an injurious mistake, you must invest the time in cultivating the relationship *before* that relationship is put to the test. Time really *is* precious.

38

Ten Words That Build Trust

Do YOU THINK one short sentence at the end of your ad could cause a major increase in the level of trust customers place in you? Believe it or not, it's true. Researchers found that placing the following statement at the end of an ad for an auto service firm caused their trust scores to jump as much as 33 percent![8]

"You can trust us to do the job for you."

Does this seem like something that shouldn't even need to be said? Clearly, the implication in any ad or relationship is that if you give the firm a job to do, it will do it. In this short sentence, there's no claim that the job will be done right, done better, done quickly, or even done with a smile.

Nevertheless, that phrase caused people to rate the firm higher in every category:

- Fair price—up 7 percent
- Caring—up 11 percent
- Fair treatment—up 20 percent
- Quality—up 30 percent
- Competency—up 33 percent

It's quite surprising that as nebulous as the "trust us" statement was, it produced major increases in very specific areas of performance.

Brainfluence Takeaway: Tell 'em to Trust You

If you want your customers to trust you, remind them that they *can* trust you. Try it. It will work. You can trust me.

39

Trust Your Customer

WANT YOUR CUSTOMERS to trust you? Show that you trust *them!* This may seem counterintuitive, but there's sound neuromarketing reasoning behind it. The concept revolves around that seemingly magical neurochemical oxytocin, which is a key factor in forming trust relationships. Paul Zak, director of the Center for Neuroeconomics Studies at Claremont Graduate University and unofficial oxytocin evangelist, relates a story about how in his younger days he was the victim of a small-scale swindle. He now concludes that a key factor in getting him to fall for the con was that the swindler demonstrated that he trusted Zak.[9]

In particular, Zak notes, our brains make us feel good when we help others. This is the reason we attach ourselves to family and friends, and even cooperate with strangers. (That's usually a good thing, unless that stranger is a con artist!)

Zak explains that this behavior is all part of what he calls THOMAS—the human oxytocin-mediated attachment system. THOMAS allows us to empathize with others and plays an important role in building social relationships.

How can this understanding help us sell more effectively? Building trust is an essential part of the sales process, and anything that we can do to foster that will pay dividends.

Brainfluence Takeaway: Show Trust to Get Trust

Building on what Zak suggests, one key way to build your customers' trust is by demonstrating that you trust *them*. (Obviously, behaving in a transparent and trustworthy manner yourself is important as well.)

How can you demonstrate trust in your customers? Here are a few ideas:

- Make a loaner/trial product available with few restrictions.
- Establish credit without lengthy forms and an onerous screening process.
- Share confidential information without making the customer sign a nondisclosure agreement.

Note that showing trust doesn't mean that you should take unnecessary business risks—just ensure your practices demonstrate that you trust the customer, and do as much of the self-protective work, like checking credit, in the background.

Depending on the relationship with the customer, you can probably think of any number of other ways to show trust. And, a customer who thinks you trust him or her will be far more likely to reciprocate.

SECTION

Seven

Brainfluence in Person

ALTHOUGH MORE AND more business is conducted remotely with ever less human-to-human interaction, there are times when we get to interact with customers in person.

In advertising, we talk about rich media and immersive ads. When you think about it, though, there's nothing richer or more immersive than person-to-person contact. Multiple senses are engaged, eye contact occurs, body language is used to send messages—these are things the human brain was designed to process. In this section, we'll see how to maximize our success when we have the increasingly rare opportunity to meet face-to-face.

40

It Pays to Schmooze

ONE OF MY all-time favorite TV commercials is the classic 1990 United Airlines spot that shows a manager distributing plane tickets to the sales staff so that they can visit their customers in person. This was filmed in the days before e-mail and the Internet, but even then phones and faxes were low-cost competition for face-to-face meetings.

That United Airlines ad worked because its story resonated with its audience. It also worked because of its acting and production values; it's a full-blown business drama packed into a 60-second commercial.

In fact, there's research that backs up United Airlines's implied claim that there's no substitute for face-to-face customer contact. Good old-fashioned face time *can* have a significant impact on trust and behavior.

Scientists love to create artificial situations to mimic the real world, and one of the classics is a setup known as the ultimatum game. In it, one participant decides how to share a sum of money (e.g., $10) with another subject. The second subject can accept or reject the split. If the split is rejected, nobody receives any money. Although classic economic theory suggests that any nonzero offer should be accepted (since even a dollar is better than nothing), real people tend to reject what they perceive as unfair offers that are too skewed toward the first subject.

In the standard ultimatum game, about half of all splits are fair—within 10 points of a 50/50 split. Although some players will behave like rational economists and accept whatever nonzero amount is offered, one third of the splits are rejected.

Researcher Al Roth tried an interesting twist on the ultimatum game: he had the subjects talk face-to-face before playing. Amazingly, even when the subjects did not discuss the game and chatted about random topics, they were far more likely to conclude the game with a successful split. With the conversation, the percentage of fair offers rose to 83 percent and a mere 5 percent of the games resulted in failure.[1]

That's a stunning difference, and it shows that establishing rapport with another person really does alter behavior.

A lab experiment at INSEAD showed similar results when wholesale/retail relationships were simulated with one player for each role. Although each player could attempt to maximize his or her own price and profit, the highest total revenue and profits could be achieved when the two parties cooperated to allow a lower market price. When the two parties established a social relationship before participating, they behaved in a more cooperative and fairer manner and achieved higher profits than pairs without a relationship.[2]

Brainfluence Takeaway: Schmooze First; Bargain Later

Don't be in too much of a rush to get down to business. Time spent chatting about kids, golf, or the upcoming weekend may seem like a waste of time, but it's laying the groundwork for mutual respect and trust. The likelihood of reaching a deal that satisfies both parties will increase.

An interesting probability is that connecting electronically via social media could have a similar effect; certainly, a full video connection like Skype or web conferencing would allow some level of face-to-face socializing. If you can't be there in person, try some electronic schmoozing to break the ice.

41

Shake Hands Like a Pro

SALES AND BUSINESS experts have always talked about the power of a handshake to make a good first impression and to start building a relationship. Research backs this up: a study at the University of Iowa showed that student job applicants with good handshakes were scored higher on employability.[3]

"Handshake experts" judged the quality of the applicants' handshakes, while recruiters rated their employability and other aspects of the applicants. Those students whose handshakes scored the best also ranked higher for employability, extroversion, and overall social skills. Applicants with limp handshakes were rated as less employable and less outgoing.

What is it about handshaking that seems to engage the emotions of the two participants? Neuroscientist and oxytocin guru Paul Zak says that touch primes the brain to release oxytocin.

How About a Nice Massage?

In one study Zak conducted, two groups of subjects participated in a game in which they exchanged money. One group received a 15-minute massage while members of the other group rested alone. The brains of the massage group released much more oxytocin. More significantly, members of the massage group returned two and a half times as much money to a trusting stranger than the control group members.[4]

Zak hypothesizes that our brains use oxytocin to unconsciously assess whether a person is trustworthy. Our brain combines our memory of past encounters and multiple sensory inputs from the current encounter. If the stranger seems to match up with people we have found to be trustworthy in the past, the brain releases oxytocin, flagging the new contact as "safe to trust."

Dopamine is released in the brain's reward center at the same time, associating a person we trust with pleasure. This speeds up processing the next time. Overall, this is how oxytocin causes most of us to be prosocial. Compassion, generosity, love, and related emotions are in part based on this cycle.

Zak's research suggests that if a firm handshake is good, a massage might be even better. That's likely true. Unfortunately, a typical job interview or sales call doesn't usually permit that kind of activity.

Brainfluence Takeaway: Touch Is Important

Oxytocin studies and other research make it clear that touch is an important tool in building trust. Typically, this means a good handshake—the Iowa researchers report that the best handshakes include "a complete, firm grip, eye contact and a vigorous up-and-down movement." Don't use a grip so firm that it causes pain.

Most business encounters allow two handshakes: one at the beginning of the meeting and one at the end. Make the most of both handshake opportunities.

More Touching?

Although additional touching—say, guiding an interviewee through a doorway—might help build the bond that Zak talks about, I'd recommend caution. Touching a stranger is a potentially risky strategy and highly dependent on cultural and personal factors. What might seem like a natural touch to some might seem odd or offensive to others. But, if appropriate, a casual touch may help build trust.

For Women Only

Another study showed that a light touch on a person's shoulder made that person more willing to choose a riskier option when deciding between accepting a sum of money or taking a chance on getting either a larger sum or nothing.[5]

Oddly, however, the shoulder touch effect worked only for female touchers. A male touch had no effect, whereas the female touch worked for both male and female subjects.

Because a purchase decision often involves some risk, such as trying a new product or changing suppliers, women might try the shoulder touch approach if the situation allows it.

A Final Caution

Not everyone likes handshakes. The most famous handshake-phobic person is real estate magnate Donald Trump. Trump said in his blog, "I think that the only thing better than a good handshake is no handshake at all. I've long said that handshakes are a bad idea because of all the germs people spread when they shake hands."

Trump would prefer that we adopt the Japanese practice of bowing. No germs, but no oxytocin, either.

42

Right Ear Selling

IF YOU WANT to get someone to do something, speak into the person's right ear. Research by Dr. Luca Tommasi and Daniele Marzoli from the University Gabriele d'Annunzio in Chieti, Italy, shows not only that we have a preference for processing spoken information via our right ear but that requests made to that ear are more likely to be successful.

In what has to be a brilliant choice of research venues, Tommasi and Marzoli decided to study ear preference in noisy nightclubs. In one study, they simply observed club patrons talking and found that almost three quarters of the interactions took place on the right side of the listener.[6]

Then, they became participants by asking other clubbers for a cigarette by speaking into the target's right or left ear. Surprisingly, they had significantly more success in cadging a smoke when they spoke into the clubber's right ear.

Brainfluence Takeaway: Favor Your Prospect's Right Ear

Naturally, most sales don't happen by yelling into one ear. Nevertheless, there are some practical applications for this research. Here are just a few:

- Dinner seating: If more than two are dining, the key sales communicator should sit to the right of the decision maker.
- Sales office layout: Although most communications in a typical sales office will be more or less face-to-face and binaural, it would be wise

to avoid any seating layouts in which the salesperson is talking to the left side of the prospect.

■ Networking events: We've all been to networking receptions, trade shows, and other events where one has to talk into someone's ear to be heard over loud music or other background noise. Although listeners will generally adjust their position to one that is comfortable, keep in mind the right-side preference when initiating a conversation. This situation is very similar to the one tested by the researchers, and they were significantly more successful when initiating contact via the right ear.

One thing that I like about this research is that it wasn't conducted in a structured, artificial lab setting but rather in a real-world venue with unsuspecting subjects. The realistic nature of the research should increase the probability of success when putting these findings into practice.

43

Smile!

What's the first thing a manager teaches a new retail or food service employee? Maybe "Don't steal the cash!" is first, but right after that is, "Smile at the customer!" It turns out that this is probably even better advice than one might think. A truly fascinating study shows that exposure to brief images of smiling or frowning faces—too quickly for the subject to consciously process—actually affected the amount people were willing to pay for a drink![7]

It's not difficult to imagine a positive, smiling staff member selling more, on average, than a scowling one. But a study done a few years ago by Piotr Winkielman of the University of California, San Diego, and Kent C. Berridge of the University of Michigan showed that even *subliminal* smile images could have a significant effect. The researchers showed subjects a picture of a neutral face that was neither smiling or unsmiling for a little less than half a second. That's long enough to recognize the face and identify its gender, which is what the subjects were supposed to do. The researchers also inserted a very brief image of a smiling or scowling face. This image was shown for only 16 milliseconds.

The subjects were unaware of the smile/scowl image they had been exposed to and were neither more nor less positive. Despite this, subjects who were thirsty served themselves more of a beverage and drank more if they saw a happy face.

The Price of a Smile

A second phase of the study showed that thirsty subjects would pay about twice as much for the same beverage if they saw a happy face instead of an angry one.

The researchers deduced that the role played by thirst showed that the emotional reactions were biopsychological in nature and were unaffected by conscious processing of the stimuli. The authors call this phenomenon *unconscious emotion*, referring to the fact that an apparent emotional change has occurred with the subject being aware of neither the stimulus that caused it nor the shift in his emotional state.

Brainfluence Takeaway: Smiles, Even Smiling Images, Help Sales

Flashing smiling subliminal images at customers waiting to be served at a burger restaurant doesn't seem very practical, or very ethical for that matter. What the study does show is that even a tiny elevation of mood, so small that it is imperceptible to the subjects, can affect customer consumption and willingness to spend.

In short, the manager who trains employees to smile is on the right track. In addition, imagery in the purchase area should be positive, and any pictured people should be smiling.

A secondary takeaway is that market researchers should be very cautious when asking people to describe their emotional state. The research showed significant behavioral effects even when the subjects did not notice any change in their emotions. Simply asking people questions inevitably fails to disclose what's really happening in their brains.

44

Confidence Sells

IS IT BETTER to know your stuff or to act like you do? If you are in the business of convincing other people, whether as a consultant, salesperson, team member, or any other position that requires others to believe you, it pays to be confident.

A study by Don Moore from Carnegie Mellon University's Center for Behavioral Decision Research showed that confidence even trumps past accuracy in earning the trust of others.[8]

Moore asked volunteers to guess the weight of people from photos. The volunteers were given cash for correct guesses and were able to buy advice from one of four other volunteers. The people guessing couldn't see what weights the other volunteers had estimated, but they could see a confidence rating for each one.

Unsurprisingly, from the very beginning, those volunteers in the advisory role sold more advice if they were confident in their estimate. As the game progressed and those guessing gained experience with the accuracy of the other volunteers, they did tend to avoid those with the most incorrect past answers. This bias, though, was more than offset by their confidence estimates. In short, confidence trumped demonstrated accuracy.

This finding may not be a huge surprise, since people naturally associate confidence with expertise. A strategy of trusting confidence breaks down, though, when someone sounds very confident without actually being right. It also means that simplistic, but confident, explanations of complex topics such as climate change and future economic behavior may find more believers than the nuanced opinion of a true expert. The latter, in the interest of accuracy and completeness, might describe multiple scenarios and the uncertainty associated with each. This makes the expert less credible than the confident person with a simple explanation.

Confidence Man: Jim Cramer

For an example of over-the-top confidence, look at *Mad Money*'s Jim Cramer (CNBC). Like any financial advisor, he has a mixed record of accuracy in his forecasts for markets and individual stocks. Nevertheless, he has his own television show and a huge following.

A big key to Cramer's success in building an audience is his confidence and appearance of expertise. When a phone call comes in with a question about a relatively obscure company, Cramer reels off the ticker symbol, gives a quick synopsis of what the company does and why he likes or doesn't like it, and gives a firm buy or sell recommendation (complete with sound effects and flashing lights). No waffling, no alternative scenarios, no neutral "hold" recommendations—just a quick demonstration of deep knowledge and a firm, unambiguous opinion. That's confidence, and it works for Cramer.

Natural Mind Readers

It's possible that mirror neurons play a role in our affinity for confident people. Studies have shown that when we interact with another person, our mirror neurons will fire sympathetically not just in response to the physical motions or gestures of the other person but also in response to his or her emotional state.[9]

This observation has led scientists to suggest that we are all natural mind readers. From an early age, we observe others and build a sort of database of emotions that lets us interpret the feelings of others. This is subconscious and automatic, and it influences our behavior. So, confidence begets confidence.

Brainfluence Takeaway: Demonstrate Confidence

Should we all become obnoxiously confident in our own opinions and never admit that other views might have merit? Of course not. But if we want to close sales, get projects approved, and achieve other objectives requiring persuasion, we need to communicate our confidence to others.

I'm not suggesting that we adopt false bravado to manipulate others. Rather, we should use time-honored strategies to develop our confidence. Salespeople should truly believe in their product. Every persuader should achieve mastery of the facts. Confidence will flow naturally from these.

Sometimes real uncertainty exists; for example, the product may not work in the particular situation, surgery might make the condition worse, or the research project may not produce a breakthrough. It would be foolish and unethical to ignore possible negative outcomes in the name of staying confident. When such uncertainty is present, describe the alternative outcomes and, if possible, assign a probability. But, if you are recommending what you believe is the best course of action, don't waffle or spend too much time discussing alternative possibilities; this will leave the audience confused and doubtful. Be honest, transparent, and confident in your recommendation.

45

Small Favors, Big Results

FROM TIME TO time, all of us need to persuade people we don't know personally to do things. A salesperson wants to close a deal. An office worker needs to persuade the new computer technician to fix her computer first. A fund-raiser hopes to get a potential donor to make a pledge. Our natural instinct in such situations is to avoid asking the individual we want to persuade for any favors other than the one that's important to us. After all, the only thing worse than being asked for a favor is being asked for multiple favors, right?

The expected and seemingly logical answer, that asking for more than one favor is unwise, is wrong. Behavioral research shows us that sometimes asking for one favor first can greatly increase the probability of success with the second favor!

Got the Time, Buddy?

My first encounter with the counterintuitive concept that asking for one favor improves the success rate when asking for a second favor was when I read about a study conducted on a city street. A researcher asked passersby for complicated directions. Not all subjects bothered to help. Some subjects were asked first for an extremely small favor: the researcher inquired as to the time of day. Virtually all of the passersby checked their watch and provided the time.

Here's the interesting part: subjects that complied with the initial small request were much more likely to respond to the more time-consuming one. The psychology seemed to be a sort of subconscious feeling that having granted one request, it would be consistent to grant a somewhat bigger one.

Signs of Success

A more recent experiment asked homeowners to display a 3′ × 6′ "Drive Carefully" sign in their front yard. Only 17 percent of homeowners in an upscale neighborhood agreed to do so, despite being offered the slightly scary assurance that the sign installers would take care of all digging needed for the holes for the support posts.[10]

Amazingly, the positive response rate increased to 76 percent among a similar group of homeowners who, two weeks earlier, had been asked to put a tiny "Safe Driver" sign in their house window. The latter request was a minor inconvenience, and virtually all homeowners agreed to it.

I find the idea that three quarters of the second group would agree to having people come out, tear up their lawn, and install a big sign quite surprising; in fact, even the 17 percent number for the first group was a bit of a surprise. That the simple step of making an insignificant earlier request more than quadrupled the response rate is truly amazing.

Foot in the Door

In another study, intrepid investigators asked people if they would be willing to allow five or six researchers to come inside their house for two hours to root through their closets and cupboards and classify the goods found for a study. An astonishing 22 percent of the households contacted agreed to this invasion of personal space—clearly, one fifth of the population is either unable to say "no" or so bored that they'll agree to anything for a break in their routine.[11]

The researchers contacted a second group of households with a request to answer a few survey questions by phone on the same topic, a simple favor to which almost all agreed. Three days later, they asked the phone survey group to participate in the invasive, time-consuming study, and the positive response rate more than doubled to 56 percent! Clearly, the initial foot-in-the-door approach of the simple survey caused many more households to throw their doors completely open for the nosy researchers.

Brainfluence Takeaway: Ask for a Small Favor First

The message in all this is clear. Making a small initial request of your targets won't turn them off. Rather, if it is small enough to be granted by almost everyone, it will make them much more likely to respond positively to your ultimate request.

Here are just a few ways to get that small initial favor:

- Ask for a cup of coffee or glass of water.
- Ask for a tiny trial order, no matter how small.
- If you are raising funds, get the donor to make a trivially small donation before you make your real pitch.
- Ask a prospect to complete a short survey.

The variety of small setup favors is endless. Regardless of which approach you adopt, that initial foot in the door will greatly increase the odds of success later.

46

Hire Articulate Salespeople

FEW WOULD ARGUE that one of the most important skills a salesperson can have is to understand what the customer is thinking, but that's a skill that's difficult to measure. Instead, hiring managers usually rely on evidence of past sales success (a good predictor of future performance) and the interview (a reasonable simulation of an in-person sales call).

Perhaps those managers hiring salespeople should consider checking the candidate's SAT Verbal score, too. A study at Wellesley College shows that advanced language skills correlate with the ability to predict what another person is thinking.[12]

The investigators conducted the experiment using deaf adults with differing degrees of signing skills. They showed the subjects a series of pictures that told part of a story, and then they asked the subjects to choose the next picture in the sequence from two choices. Correct predictions would be based on what the character in the story was thinking. The subjects who had more advanced signing ability were better able to choose the correct picture.

One might guess that the advanced signers were smarter and hence better able to interpret the story, but, in fact, individuals who learned better signing skills over a period of time also improved their ability to predict the story character's thought process.

Brainfluence Takeaway: Hire Articulate People

The researchers determined that advanced language skills are required to fully utilize our innate ability to understand what other people are thinking. So, hiring an articulate salesperson (or manager, customer service person, and so on) may have a dual benefit: not only will that individual make a better impression on customers and others, but he or she may be better able to read the customer's state of mind.

47

You're the Best!

YOUR MOTHER PROBABLY told you, "Flattery will get you nowhere."

Mom was wrong. Research shows that even when people perceive that flattery is insincere, that flattery can still leave a lasting and positive impression of the flatterer.

Elaine Chan and Jaideep Sengupta of the Hong Kong University of Science and Technology found that even insincere flattery can have a persuasive influence on consumers, despite their efforts to correct for the flatterer's motive. According to Chan and Sengupta, even when we realize we are being flattered, and "correct" for that when we think about the flatterer, there is still an underlying positive impression that can be strong and long lasting. This subconscious positive impression—the researchers call it implicit—was found to influence behavior even when the subjects consciously realized that the flattery was insincere.

It's scary that we can be manipulated this easily and that our own defenses against such manipulation are ineffective even when we realize what is happening. But is there a way that ethical marketers can apply this knowledge? The answer is, "Yes!"

Brainfluence Takeaway: Use Ethical Flattery

The key to using flattery in a nonmanipulative way is to be honest. Particularly in a direct sales environment, the salesperson can praise some action or characteristic of the customer and do so in a way that is not dishonest at all. Indeed, flattery based on truth is likely to be more credible to and better received by the customer than a compliment that is blatantly false or overstated.

Mass Flattery

In marketing situations other than one-on-one interactions, you can still stay honest by using targeted pitches. For example, "As an owner of a Platinum Class suit, you showed you are an individual who can recognize sophisticated styling and superb quality . . ."

These customized approaches are more honest and likely far more effective than, say, a mass mailing that makes a generic flattering statement about the recipient. Even though the research suggests that generic flattery might work even if the recipient discounted it as insincere, statements grounded in truth will cause less cognitive dissonance and create a more favorable impression of the company and brand.

48

Coffee, Anyone?

IF YOU'RE MEETING with a sales prospect in person for the first time, think twice before you offer the person a nice, ice-cold beverage. Instead, try a steaming mug of hot coffee to make the best impression. One of my favorite researchers, John Bargh of Yale University, found that the temperature of a beverage makes a difference in how one person judges another person.[13]

An experiment gave subjects cups of either iced or hot coffee and then told them to rate someone else's personality solely from a file of information about that person. Which group do you think scored the person higher for "warmth"? The hot coffee group, of course!

The researchers attribute this effect to the fact that brain imaging studies show hot and cold stimuli light up an area of the brain related to trust and cooperation.

Interestingly enough, the warm beverages affect not just our perceptions of other people but our own behavior as well. According to Bargh, "Physical warmth can make us see others as warmer people, but also cause us to be warmer—more generous and trusting—as well."

Brainfluence Takeaway: Serve Hot Beverages

Given the choice, you might be better off meeting a sales prospect or potential business partner for coffee than a cold drink. Not only will your companion judge *you* to be a warmer person, he or she will be more generous and trusting as well.

(Unfortunately, the researchers did not conduct variations on the experiment using alcoholic beverages, which, I have heard from reliable sources, have their own behavior modification potential! Hot toddies, anyone?)

To really carry the strategy to an extreme, a hot beverage in a non-insulated mug that needs to be held in one's hand would seem to be the best approach. Perhaps the reason Chinese restaurants serve a pot of tea with little handle-free cups is to spread warm feelings around the table!

Memory Bonus

As a plus for serving a caffeinated beverage, caffeine has been shown to boost short-term memory.[14] So, not only will your pitch be better received, it may be more memorable, too.

49

Candy Is Dandy

COULD EATING A chocolate treat make you want to buy a TV or book a cruise? The surprising answer is, "YES!"

At a mall I used to frequent, there was a candy kiosk that always offered a sample chocolate to each passerby. I wondered about the economics of that practice—it seemed that almost everyone grabbed the treat and kept on walking—but I assumed that it must be profitable or they wouldn't keep doing it.

In fact, tempting an individual and getting him or her to indulge will actually increase the person's desire to keep indulging. Even more surprising, the desire to indulge goes far beyond having another piece of candy and extends to high-priced consumer items such as fancy computers and designer shirts!

Researchers Julio Laran of Miami University and Chris Janiszewski of the University of Florida offered subjects a chocolate truffle and encouraged them to eat it. They found that the subjects who indulged were eager to keep indulging, not only consuming more truffles but also fatty foods such as ice cream, pizza, and chips.[15]

That might not seem odd—there's certainly a grain of truth in the old Lay's Potato Chip slogan, "Betcha can't eat just one!" But the truly startling finding was that the desire to indulge expanded to much more than tasty treats.

An additional experiment found that subjects who ate the first truffle also assigned more value to consumer goods such as Apple computers, designer shirts, high-end TVs, and cruises compared with those subjects who successfully resisted the truffle temptation.

There were a few other relevant findings as well. First, if the subjects continued to consume truffles until satisfied, the desire to indulge turned off. Second, those individuals who resisted the truffle also seemed to become more virtuous in their attempts to avoid self-indulgence.

Brainfluence Takeaway: Try the Truffle Strategy

Should you tempt your customers with some kind of indulgent treat? If you sell a product that might be considered an indulgence, such as a premium or luxury item or a product that people want but don't need, the truffle strategy might work. But don't keep feeding them treats, or their desire to indulge themselves will fade. Also, be aware that those customers who resist the temptation may actually become harder to sell to.

Thinking back to the chocolate kiosk in the mall, I wonder now if the mall operator or surrounding merchants should have subsidized the free chocolates. The delivery mechanism was just about perfect: The clerk offered each passerby one sample, so there was no opportunity for a sweet-toothed customer to grab a handful. The samples were small enough that just about everyone who accepted one wanted more. (No doubt that was the chocolatier's strategy.) But, according to these findings, each customer who accepted and ate one of the tasty morsels was primed to spend more money—and not just for a box of chocolates!

50

Selling Secrets of Magicians

IF YOU THINK that magicians and neuroscientists have little to talk about, you'd be wrong: both deal with issues like attention and consciousness, albeit in different ways. Marketers can learn from both professions and, in particular, from understanding how magicians can fool us even when we are trying to pay attention.[16]

Here are a few ways that magicians exploit our mental processes that can be used by marketers—not to trick customers, but to better engage them and hold their attention:

1. People Focus on Only One Thing

I consider myself a multitasker, and no doubt most businesspeople would say the same about themselves. But the success of stage magicians shows that we can only *really* pay attention to one thing at a time. Many illusions are based on the magician showing you something with one hand while doing something you don't notice with the other hand.

Neuroscientists compare our attention focus to shining a spotlight on something: we see what is lit, and we lose focus on everything else. The term *tunnel vision* is particularly apt to describe how people zero in on one small area at a time.

Marketers need to be sure they have focused their target's attention where they want it. If the customer is distracted by something external, or worse, by something else the salesperson is doing (or that is happening in an advertisement), the key point of the pitch will be missed.

Magic Strategy #1: Don't let (or make) your customers multitask when you need their attention on your message!

2. Motion Attracts Our Attention

Ever wonder why doves are such popular props with magicians? I'm sure their docile nature and willingness to tolerate being stuffed in a pocket are important, but the explosive burst of white, flapping wings as they fly off is guaranteed to draw every eyeball in the audience. The ability of the birds to hijack the viewers' attention gives the performer a window of opportunity to set up the next stage of the illusion.

Our brains are wired to respond to motion—after all, in prehistoric times, movement might be a threat, or perhaps food. Magicians exploit that response in many ways, and you can too.

Magic Strategy #2: Whether you are presenting to a group, selling one-on-one, or designing a TV commercial, use motion to grab the attention of your audience and focus it where you want it. If there's one thing that's moving, that's where the audience will look.

3. Big Motions Beat Little Motions

If you were watching a magician standing on the stage and he or she made a small, quick move to his or her pocket, you would likely notice it. Magicians know that and prevent you from seeing their small moves by distracting you with a big move, such as pulling a colorful scarf out of a pocket in a sweeping gesture with their other hand. They know the audience will tune out the small move in favor of paying attention to the big one.

Magic Strategy #3: If you are dealing with an audience who is distracted or who may be losing focus, use *big* motions to snap them to attention.

4. The Unexpected Attracts Us

When I watch a magician, I always try to pay close attention to spot any shady moves. So does the rest of the audience. It's rare to spot a skilled magician's tricks, though—not just because of the distraction techniques described previously. Magicians hide some of their moves by making them look like expected actions.

For example, when magicians scratch their ears, shoot their cuffs, or make other moves we are familiar with, our brains tune it out as expected and uninteresting. That move may well mask a transfer of a prop or some other preparation step. On the other hand, if magicians were to place their palms on top of their heads or raise their left arm for no apparent reason, we'd all be watching carefully.

Novelty attracts us; the routine bores us.

Magic Strategy #4: To get your customers' attention, surprise them with an unexpected move, a novel sound, or an unfamiliar image. That will cause them to look at and analyze what they are seeing. That's true even with text—"New!" is one of the most attention-getting words in advertising.

5. Mirror Neurons Engage Us

One reason we don't notice when magicians scratch their noses while slyly palming a coin that was hidden in their mouth is that we *know* what it feels like to scratch our noses. When magicians engage in that activity, if we notice at all, our mirror neurons are lighting up as if we were performing that action ourselves.

Magicians exploit this phenomenon with decoy actions—appearing to take a drink, for example, but really passing an item from mouth to hand in the process. Our brains aid the deception by playing along with the decoy activity and interpreting the action as one we are already wired to understand.

Magic Strategy #5: Even though marketers aren't normally trying to disguise sneaky actions, there is a lesson here. When people see someone performing a familiar action, either in person or on video, their brains will engage as their mirror neurons kick in. Selling soft drinks? Let people experience opening the bottle, raising it to their lips, and taking a drink. Magicians know how familiar physical actions engage our brain, and you should too.

6. Cut the Chatter

If you've ever been to a magic show, either on a stage or close-up, you know that the magician often keeps talking. Good magicians will talk about what they are doing, why it is difficult, and so on, while their hands are busy with the trick. Their purpose, of course, is not to give you real information about their technique but rather to distract you. In essence, the magician's patter is another stream of information for your brain to process, and the overload makes it less likely that you will spot what is really happening.

Magic Strategy #6: While a stream of chatter serves the magician's purposes, talking too much can distract your customers from your selling points. Have you ever encountered a salesperson who wouldn't shut up while you were examining a product? It's hard to look at, say, a car's control panel, while a salesperson is spouting a stream of inane babble.

Salespeople should be trained not just what to say, but when to say it—and when not to say anything at all. In other media, such as commercials, be aware that the spoken audio content shouldn't conflict with important information on the screen.

Even PowerPoint jockeys can learn from magicians' patter—lengthy text bullets in a presentation are a perfect example of distraction. Trying to read the text while the speaker is making the same point verbally causes low comprehension and recall because the brain is too distracted to do a good job with either task.

Brainfluence Takeaway: Learn From Magicians

Magic has likely been around in some form at least as long as marketing, and marketers would do well to learn from its practitioners! Skilled magicians are experts in holding the attention of their audiences and can direct that attention at will. In addition, magicians are masters of distraction and provide an important lesson in what *not* to do if you want your audience focused.

51

Soften Up Your Prospects

If the last time you bought a car the salesperson offered you a soft, comfortable chair, there are two possible explanations:

1. The salesperson was genuinely concerned about your comfort during a stressful negotiation.
2. The salesperson knew you would pay more than if you sat in a hard chair.

The second choice sounds crazy, right? I'm sure all of us would swear that the firmness of our chair would have absolutely no effect on how much we'd pay for a car. If anything, a hard seat might make us eager to strike a deal more quickly, perhaps leaving money on the table.

The opposite is true.

A study by Joshua M. Ackerman (MIT), Christopher C. Nocera (Harvard), and John Bargh (Yale), showed that "hard objects increased rigidity in negotiations." One of a series of experiments involved a simulated car price negotiation in which the subject had to make a price offer for a car, which was rejected. Then, the "buyer" had to make a second offer. The subjects were also asked to evaluate their negotiating partner.[17]

The researchers found that there was a significant difference between subjects sitting in hard and soft chairs. Those seated in hard chairs judged their negotiating partner to be less emotional. Most significantly, the "buyers" in soft chairs *increased their offer by nearly 40 percent more* than those in hard chairs. In short, not only did a hard chair change the buyers' perception of their negotiating partners, it made them harder bargainers.

Another experiment had subjects feel a hard block of wood or a soft blanket before rating a boss-employee interaction. The subjects who felt the hard block rated the employee as being more rigid than those who felt the blanket. Will these laboratory findings translate into real-world results? Study author Joshua Ackerman says, "I suspect that the stresses of real-world decision-making environments will act as mental distracters, making people even more susceptible to the effects of tactile cues."

Brainfluence Takeaway: Soften Up Your Prospects

If you want to be perceived as more flexible in dealing with prospects while at the same time increasing their flexibility in reaching a deal, take these steps:

- Seat them in a soft chair.
- If you hand them anything, avoid hard objects.
- Offer them a warm beverage (see Chapter 48).

The combined effect will let you relate better emotionally to your prospect and will increase the chance of reaching a deal. In fact, unless you want to encourage rigidity in the people you meet with, you might make *all* your office seating soft.

SECTION

Eight

Brainfluence for a Cause

WE THINK OF marketing as being exclusively a business activity, but it extends to every type of organization—nonprofits and charities, government agencies, and education.

The concepts in this section all have particular applicability to nonprofit activity, but it's still worth a read for you for-profit marketers. Every business has times when it needs to cultivate emotions such as generosity, altruism, and socially appropriate behavior.

52

Mirror, Mirror on the Wall

HERE'S A PREDICTION: in the coming years, we'll see mirrors popping up in the entryways of churches and other places of worship—and the reason won't be to let those entering fix their hair.

The mirror has a rather magical effect on us.

Motivation experts have often told their audiences to look in the mirror as they formulated their goals or imagined the future they wanted. As it turns out, this advice wasn't all motivational hokum. When we look in a mirror, our behavior is actually altered—at least for a short period of time.[1]

The most venerable piece of mirror-behavior research dates all the way back to the 1970s. Like many experiments in social psychology, the setup was simple: children making their Halloween rounds were told they could take one piece of candy from a large bowl of candy and were then left alone. About 34 percent helped themselves to more than one piece. When a mirror was placed behind the bowl so that the children could see themselves as they took the candy, only 9 percent disobeyed their instructions. The simple addition of the mirror cut the rate of bad behavior by almost three-fourths!

And it's not just kids who respond to seeing themselves. Another experiment showed subjects either a live video of themselves (rather like looking in a mirror except for the image reversal part) or neutral geometric shapes. They were then given a small task that required them to exit the room with a used paper towel. Almost half of the subjects who saw the neutral images littered by dropping the used towel in an empty stairwell, whereas only one quarter of those who saw themselves did so.

It seems that seeing one's image causes one to think about one's behavior and ultimately behave in a more socially desirable way. According to influence and persuasion expert Robert Cialdini, other actions, such as asking people their names, can have a similar effect. Another experiment showed that a picture of eyes dramatically reduced "theft" in a break area where employees were supposed to drop money in a jar when they had a cup of coffee or tea.

Cialdini notes that mirrors could be an inexpensive way to cut shoplifting and employee theft in areas that can't readily be monitored. (No doubt they would be particularly effective if they were accompanied by a sign that said "Two-way mirrors in use.")

Brainfluence Takeaway: Let Donors See Themselves

I think there could be some interesting nonprofit marketing applications for this self-awareness strategy. Generally, charities are seeking commitments of money or time for a cause that most people would consider socially beneficial. What better way to boost their success rate than letting potential donors see themselves?

If a solicitation is taking place in an environment controlled by the nonprofit, one or more strategically placed mirrors (such as in the waiting room or behind the solicitor's desk) could work to increase the close rate and perhaps boost the average commitment. Of course, relatively few nonprofits have the luxury of bringing donors into their environment.

I think there are applications for this research in the most common way of soliciting contributions: direct mail. One would be to include an inexpensive reflective area on part of the solicitation, perhaps accompanied by wording that urged the reader to "imagine the good you could do . . ." Although the image quality might not be as good as a real mirror, the thought would be there. Personalizing the pitch by printing the donor's name below the reflective area would likely help as well.

Building on the video results, it's possible a photo of the donor could influence generosity. More costly solicitations aimed at individual large donors could even incorporate a real mirror in some way.

The benefits of using mirrors or other self-images will most likely be greatest for marketers who are clearly on the side of what is socially desirable: charities, universities, green marketers, and so on.

53

Get Closer to Heaven

IN OUR LANGUAGE, we tend to associate height with good. Heaven is above us, Hell is somewhere beneath us. God appears on a mountain, not in a valley or a well. You look up to someone you admire and look down on someone undesirable.

Not only is this association of height with good rooted in our subconscious mind, but our physical location actually affects our behavior.

Lifting Generosity

A study led by Lawrence Sanna of the University of North Carolina at Chapel Hill looked at how the physical position of subjects changed the probability that they would engage in prosocial acts, that is, do good things. One experiment involved asking mall shoppers for a charitable contribution immediately after they had gone up an escalator or gone down an escalator. They found that 16 percent of the people going up contributed, more than twice the 7 percent contributed by subjects going down. A control group of shoppers walking on level ground not near any escalators contributed at an 11 percent rate.[2]

Elevating Cooperation

Another experiment used a more controlled setting with randomly assigned subjects. Those who had gone up a set of steps spent 68 percent longer helping the experiment leader with a task than those who had gone down a set of steps.

Physical location isn't an essential component of the high/low effect. In yet another experiment, subjects saw videos shot from an airplane or a car and asked to imagine themselves in the video. They then engaged in an activity in which they thought they were helping another individual in a computer game. Subjects who saw the airplane video (the "high" position) were *60 percent more cooperative* than subjects who saw the car video (the "low" position).

Practical Implications

Since nonprofits depend on altruistic behavior to get donations and volunteers, many applications spring to mind. Locating donation tables at the top of steps or escalators would be an obvious step as it directly mimics the experiment. These findings might influence office location, too. Volunteers who walked up a flight of steps might well work harder and longer. Although not demonstrated by the experiment, I think it likely that there is a "high office" effect. Get donors into an upper-floor office with big windows or to a fund-raiser in a venue with an expansive view, and their generosity might be increased.

Business Applications

Most businesses don't run on altruism, but cooperation is important. Using the altitude effect might be a great addition to a team-building exercise or a way to encourage everyone to pitch in for an important rush project.

The researchers didn't study how long lasting the effect was, but I would suspect that repeated exposure to an elevated environment would reduce its impact. If you climb a flight of steps (or ride an elevator to the 20th floor) every day, it seems likely that the behavior effects would decline as the change in elevation became routine.

Brainfluence Takeaway: Control Altitude, Change Attitude

Where's your office? Where are you holding your next fund-raiser? Where are you meeting your customer for lunch? Keep altitude in mind. And if you are stuck in the basement, note that in one experiment merely showing the subjects a video taken from on high was enough to kick in the height effect; consider installing a mural of clouds or a big aerial photo.

54

Child Labor

WE ALL LIKE to look at images of babies (see page 86), but in addition to their fascination for most adults, they have an extra power: baby pictures can boost altruistic behavior.

An experiment in Edinburgh began by planting hundreds of wallets on city streets. Almost half were mailed back to the "owner." Most wallets contained one of four possible photos: a smiling baby, a cute puppy, a happy family, or an elderly couple. Other wallets had no photo at all, and some had charity papers inside.[3]

The results were quite startling. Fully 88 percent of the wallets with the baby photo were returned. The next best rate was the puppy photo, at 53 percent. A family photo netted a 48 percent return rate, while an elderly couple picture scored only 28 percent. Just one out of seven of the no-photo wallets was returned.

According to the principal researcher, Dr. Richard Wiseman, the high rate of return for the wallets that included a baby photo reflects an evolution-driven instinct to help vulnerable infants. Humans, in order to protect future generations, are wired to help babies, even the progeny of others.

Brainfluence Takeaway: Use Babies to Boost Altruism

For a nonprofit organization that depends on altruistic behavior, employing baby images could get donors in a more generous mood. Some groups will be better able to use the technique than others; a symphony, for example, might find it difficult to build a baby image into a fund-raising letter without it looking odd. Charities serving families, though, might consider a prominent baby picture instead of an image showing an entire family group or pictures of older children.

For-Profit Advertisers

Is there a takeaway for for-profit advertisers? At the simplest level, advertisers have long incorporated baby images simply because they grabbed the viewer's attention. Perhaps in some cases they got an altruistic boost, too.

The general categories of safety and protection might benefit from the baby effect. Michelin, the tire maker, pictured a baby next to a tire in an ad that emphasized the safety characteristics of the product. You might be willing to risk your own neck driving on cheap tires, but would you take a chance with that cute baby?

Life insurance is another example of a product that might be ignored until framed in the context of providing for one's family, and in particular, for a helpless infant.

55

Give Big, Get Bigger

RECIPROCITY IS A recurring theme in discussions of influencing behavior. The concept of reciprocity suggests that giving someone something, or doing a favor for someone, establishes a subtle return obligation. An interesting study by German researcher Armin Falk showed that a bigger gift amplifies the reciprocity effect. Falk's study involved mailing 10,000 requests for charitable donations, divided into three groups. One group received only the letter requesting the donation, one group received the letter plus a free postcard and envelope (the small gift), and the last group received a package containing four postcards and envelopes (the large gift).[4]

The idea that sending a gift along with a charitable donation request boosts response is well established, and the experiment bore this out: the small gift boosted donation totals by 17 percent. The recipients of the large gift, though, were even more generous: they donated 75 *percent more* than the no-gift group.

This experiment is significant in a couple of ways. First, it tested reciprocity in the real world, not in an academic setting with undergrads used as inexpensive lab rats. Second, it demonstrated that the reciprocity effect is proportional to the perceived size of the gift or favor, even when the variations are relatively minor.

Nonprofit Reciprocity Strategy

Nonprofits are well aware of the reciprocity effect, and they use it to great advantage. Some use an approach nearly identical to the test, mailing unsolicited small gifts such as address labels or holiday cards to boost donation rates. This research shows that testing different gift values and types is extremely important.

Clearly, four cards had passed some kind of tipping point that spiked donations compared with those generated when a single card was used. But would two cards have done nearly as well? Would six cards have caused enough of an increase to justify the even higher cost? And what if the cards were of exceptional quality (and apparently higher value) or if the gift was something other than cards?

The great thing about direct mail is that it lends itself to testing. It's easy to segment donor lists for different mailings and to track the response rate for each package. With a little investment in testing and gift options, a nonprofit can determine whether a bigger gift will boost the donation rate by more than enough to cover the added cost.

Business Reciprocity

Although businesses don't send gifts to potential customers asking for donations, a reciprocity strategy can still work. (Conference swag is one example; give away a T-shirt or a gimmicky pen, and many booth visitors will feel an obligation to listen to your pitch.)

One business use of direct mail that is somewhat similar to Falk's experiment is the "appointment request" letter often used in sales prospecting. The typical letter introduces the salesperson, mentions the business purpose (e.g., showing the customer how to save money on insurance), perhaps mentions a shared personal connection, and suggests meeting in person. A business that uses this approach should try increasing their appointment-setting success with the inclusion of a small gift for the recipient. Not only will reciprocity kick in, but the mailing piece will stand out from the flood of other mail on the recipient's desk.

Brainfluence Takeaway: Gift Your Prospects

Reciprocity is a potent force, and it makes sense to try varying gifts to accompany your appeal. Even a minor change in the gift may have a significant impact on the response rate, and the only way to determine the most cost-effective strategy is to test.

The old maxim says, "It's better to give than to receive." The reciprocity effect might change this to, "It's best to give, and then receive!"

56

Make It Personal

LOGIC TELLS US that a bigger problem should get more attention. One person suffering from a disease is certainly bad, but a thousand afflicted individuals should motivate us far more. As is often the case in our odd world of neuromarketing, research shows that our brains operate in an illogical and perhaps unexpected manner.

Paul Slovic, a researcher at Decision Research, demonstrated this by measuring the contribution levels from people shown pictures of starving children. Some subjects were shown a photo of a single starving child from Mali; others were shown a photo of two children. All were identified by name. The subjects shown two children donated 15 percent less than those shown the single child. In a related experiment, subjects shown a group of eight starving children contributed 50 percent less money than those shown just one.[5]

This tendency may be hardwired. We are drawn to stories about one person in crisis (a great example was the national fascination with Baby Jessica, who was trapped in a well), but mass starvation or rampant disease barely engages us.

Clearly, nonprofit marketers need to make their marketing efforts as personal as possible—and not just on the donor side, but on the recipient side as well. This is real one-to-one marketing.

No charity understands the concept better than ChildFund International (formerly Christian Children's Fund), who lets its donors sponsor a single child identified by name, photo, and other personal details. Potential donors see a photo and biography of a child they can sponsor; the cost is made to appear minimal by expressing it in "cents a day."

A typical description begins like this: "Sindy is a pretty little girl who lives in a poor rural community located in the western part of Honduras, Central America. She stays healthy most of the time and has no physical impediments. Sindy attends preschool. She likes drawing and playing with dolls . . ." There is also a photo that shows a needy but not pathetic child.

Furthermore, if you aren't moved to save that particular child from abject poverty, you can click a link for "Search for a different child" that lets you see several new child photos and also lets you search by gender, age, and other factors in case you have a preference. The potential donor can project his or her own needs onto a seemingly limitless database of needy children, browsing them until the perfect match comes up.

I'm in no way criticizing the great work ChildFund does—I was a donor for many years myself. But this is absolutely brilliant marketing! Their approach, which we now find has a sound basis in behavioral research, helps explain why ChildFund has been around for 70 years and, according to their data, has helped more than 15 million children.

Another powerful element of ChildFund's personalized recipient approach is that most donors no doubt feel obligated to keep giving; even if you cut back donations to other charities, do you really want to imagine "your child" being tossed back into a life of grinding poverty because you wanted to make a few more Starbucks runs each month? I'd guess ChildFund's donor continuity numbers are off the charts compared with that of other charities.

Brainfluence Takeaway: Make It Personal

Most nonprofits can benefit from a more personal approach to describing the recipients of their largesse. Don't contribute to the symphony's general fund; sponsor a cellist named Marie. Don't just write a check to the university you graduated from, provide an incoming freshman from Iowa with the aid she needs to enable her to attend. Many nonprofits have discovered the power of personalizing their appeal already, but others still inundate potential owners with mind-numbing statistics.

Nonprofit marketers would do well to remember that the vast majority of their donors aren't adept at converting statistics into a donation strategy and that our brains are wired to respond more strongly to an individual plight than the same condition afflicting a group. Appeals personalized for individual donors have always been important in raising money, but personalizing the recipients can be just as important.

57

Lose the Briefcase!

MOST NONPROFIT ORGANIZATIONS try to present as businesslike an appearance as possible. After all, donors want to know their contributions will be handled properly. Looking organized is fine, but specific cues could actually cause donors to be more stingy.

Researchers at Stanford and Yale universities showed subjects either pictures of objects from the world of business (briefcases, boardroom tables, fountain pens, dress shoes, business suits, etc.) or neutral pictures (kites, electrical sockets, turkeys, whales, sheet music, etc.).

When the subjects then participated in the ultimatum game, those primed with business images behaved in a more self-serving and competitive manner. In fact, whereas 91 percent of the participants who had been shown neutral images proposed an even split of the money, just 33 percent of the business-primed group did so.[6]

To see if real objects would cause different behavior than pictures, a second test exposed one group of subjects to a briefcase, a leather portfolio, and an executive-style pen. The experimenter withdrew a form from the briefcase and told each subject to place the completed form in the portfolio. A control group received similar instructions but the business objects were replaced with a backpack, a cardboard box, and a common wooden pencil.

Once again, the business-primed subjects demonstrated a selfish streak. Whereas 100 percent of the backpack group proposed an even split of money in the ultimatum game, a mere 50 percent of the briefcase subjects were so generous.

Brainfluence Takeaway: Avoid Business and Financial Cues

When you are getting ready to ask for a donation, avoid obvious business cues and any images or objects that suggest money. For an in-person donation request, use a neutral, perhaps homelike, setting instead of an office with computers, file cabinets, and all the other trappings of business. Of course, as we saw earlier, you should also avoid all specific money or currency imagery (see page 9).

In addition, a more casual dress code makes sense. Instead of a business suit, snappy attaché case, and Montblanc pen, adopt a more relaxed look.

Negotiations, Too

Even for-profit firms can employ this strategy. A typical deal meeting might be a bunch of suits in a boardroom—this is the opposite of what you need to incite cooperation. So, just like a nonprofit hoping to spur a generous donation, get rid of as many obvious trappings of business as you can. In fact, by encouraging casual dress for all parties and holding the session in a venue less formal than a corporate boardroom, both sides will be primed for cooperation instead of competition.

58

Ask Big!

Years ago, when *The Tonight Show* ruled late-night TV and when all the guests weren't celebrities promoting their latest book, movie, or TV show, host Johnny Carson interviewed the Girl Scout who sold the most cookies that year. This young lady, Markita Andrews, set a cookie sales record that was never broken. What was her technique? In addition to hard work, she used a framing strategy to make her customers view the purchase as a trivial expense.

Markita's strategy was simple. When she knocked on a door, she would first ask for a $30,000 donation to the Girl Scouts. Naturally, she had no takers on that request. But then she'd ask if they would at least buy a box of Girl Scout cookies, and just about everyone would.[7]

This isn't unlike sticker price framing, where the list price of a product greatly exceeds the actual sale price, making the latter look like a bargain. In Markita's case, though, the strategy was a little different. By throwing out the $30,000 number, she made the few bucks for some cookies seem trivial. (I'm sure the fact that the message was delivered by a charming little girl helped as well!)

Brainfluence Takeaway: Start With a *Big* Number

Even if you aren't a precocious eight-year old, there's a real-world strategy here. If you can introduce a large number into the fund-raising or sales process, a much smaller ask amount will be cast in a better light. Try it out. You won't get on TV talk shows, but you might score a donation or close a sale.

SECTION

Nine

Brainfluence Copywriting

THE ADAGE SAYS a picture is worth a thousand words, but don't tell that to a skilled copywriter. Direct marketers, in particular, know that the right copy can increase the response rate of an offer by many multiples.

Even with today's emphasis on media that bombard the senses with motion and sound, words still pack a punch. Sophisticated language skills set humans apart from other species, and brainy marketers know that the right words can tap into customer emotions and hold their attention while conveying a message.

Our knowledge of how our brains work is now helping us understand why some copy techniques outperform others and can help *you* craft copy like a pro!

59

Surprise the Brain

NEUROSCIENTISTS ARE GETTING closer to understanding how we are surprised by unexpected events. Researchers in the United Kingdom found that the hippocampus, a small structure in our brain, "predicts" what will happen next by automatically recalling an entire sequence of events in response to a single cue.

The subjects saw a series of four images in fixed order. When the order of the final two was changed, observed activity in the hippocampus surged. The researchers concluded that the subjects' brains were predicting what would come next and, when an unexpected image appeared, the reaction occurred.[1]

There's research that sheds light on how your brain predicts what's coming next. In some cases, your brain acts like a smart word processor that suggests words you might want as you begin to type them.[2]

This text is from an audio podcast by Scientific American's Steve Mirsky[3]:

> While I'm talking, you're not just passively listening. Your brain is also busy at work, guessing the next word that I will sa . . . vor before I actually speak it. You thought I was gonna say "say," didn't you? Our brains actually consider many possible words—and their meanings— before we've heard the final sound of the word in quest . . . of being understood.

I know *my* brain anticipated "say" and "question" in the two spots where Mirsky surprised listeners with an unexpected word!

Advertising copywriters have for years used a similar technique to jar the reader out of complacency. Once in a while, they substitute an unexpected word in a familiar phrase. For example, instead of "a stitch in time saves nine," the writer might use the unexpected phrase, "a stitch in time saves money." The unexpected word at the end of a familiar phrase snaps the reader to attention.

If you want to wake up your readers or listeners, substitute an unexpected word for the one their brains have already filled in.

Brainfluence Takeaway: Surprise the Audience

This research underscores how an advertiser can get a reaction by doing something unexpected. If you present a viewer with a familiar image or situation, that person's brain will automatically predict what will happen next. If the advertiser inserts an unexpected image, word, or event, it will grab the audience's attention to a much greater degree than had the predictable occurred.

In a spoken or audio presentation, a word with a similar beginning might be particularly effective, as the brain's word-winnowing method reinforces the expectation.

The brain is constantly predicting and comparing, and providing it with something other than it predicted will cause a reaction. Make a commitment to testing this technique, because we all know that actions speak louder than . . . doing nothing!

60

Use a Simple Slogan

WE THINK OF brands as amazingly powerful. People prefer whatever cola they are drinking, as long as it's labeled Coke. People pay lots more for a Ralph Lauren polo shirt than a store-brand shirt of identical quality. Although the brand name rarely changes, brand slogans are treated as ephemeral and tend to be updated much more frequently. But, to resurrect an old Coke motto, what if a brand's slogan was *the real thing?*

Think of a brand that is all about saving money... How about Walmart? Surprising research shows that consumers exposed to the Walmart name might actually spend less than those exposed to the store's current slogan, "Save money. Live better." This curious finding was replicated with other stores and slogans by a team of researchers from Miami, Hong Kong, and Berkeley.[4]

The experiment divided subjects into two groups. Half were exposed to brand names associated with saving money, like Walmart, Dollar General, Sears, and Ross. The other half were exposed to the slogans for those retailers, such as Sears's current motto, "The Good Life at a Great Price. Guaranteed." When asked to visualize a shopping trip and describe how much money would be spent, the brand-exposed group spent an average of $94 versus the slogan group, who spent just about twice as much: $184.

A second study found that exposing consumers to a "savings" message caused them to spend more than when they saw a "luxury" message.

The researchers found the fact that a savings message caused higher spending counterintuitive and perhaps worrisome. Of course, most retailers won't be overly troubled by this incongruity. They push savings-oriented slogans not to rein in excess consumer spending, but rather to increase their own sales and gain market share.

I'd weight this research more if it had been conducted with real customers spending real money in real stores. But the findings do suggest that a savings-oriented slogan might be a way to boost sales for value brands. Most of us *are* willing to spend more if we think we are getting a deal (like that gallon of mayo in your fridge from a Sam's Club trip two years ago).

Brainfluence Takeaway: Use a Simple Savings Slogan

Perhaps we haven't been giving slogans enough credit for conveying a savings message. (Walmart, no slouch at building sales, apparently believes in the power of slogans; unlike many retailers, they build their slogan into their logo!)

The main lesson is that slogans that promise savings offer the potential to increase consumer purchases. If your brand is a value brand, develop a simple slogan and make it a centerpiece of your marketing efforts.

61

Write Like Shakespeare

FEW WOULD ARGUE that Shakespeare is one of the greatest writers in the English language, but we don't see Madison Avenue putting much of their copy in sonnet form. And although I don't expect to see a surge in the use of iambic pentameter in print ads, it turns out that Shakespeare may have something to teach twenty-first-century advertising copywriters. Neuroscience researchers at the University of Liverpool found that reading Shakespeare causes positive activation of the brain.

Using three different types of brain scans, researchers monitored brain activity in subjects as they read Shakespeare. They found that when Shakespeare used a linguistic technique called functional shift (using one part of speech for another in one such shift, for example, turning a noun into a verb), it spiked the brain activity of the reader. In essence, the reader was jolted into having to work out what Shakespeare was trying to say.[5] A phrase like "he godded me" is an example of this creative misuse of common words that causes the burst of brain activity.

Neil Roberts, one of the researchers, compares the effect of this technique to a magic trick. The momentary confusion created is positive, he says, and the spike occurs when the brain encounters the unexpected word. He attributes the long-lasting appeal of Shakespeare to the way his words engage the brain of the reader (or listener).

Brainfluence Takeaway: "Misuse" a Word

Take a lesson from the bard and shake up the way you use your words. Take a word that people know, and use it in an unexpected way. Neuro your copy!

Even if your advertising prose doesn't end up being taught in literature classes centuries from now, it may do a better job of selling today!

62

A Muffin by Any Other Name . . .

MOST OF US don't give much thought to what we call our product, at least in terms of its category. Toothpaste is toothpaste. Cars are cars. Perhaps it's time that other businesses learn what many restauranteurs already know: what you call a product affects its perceived characteristics and its sales.

Savvy eatery operators know unhealthy dishes that consumers might avoid can be made more appealing with a little creative renaming. Potato chips can be relabeled as "veggie chips," while a pasta/vegetable combination will appear more healthful if it is called a "salad." My personal favorite is the rebranding of cake as a "muffin." None of us would order carrot cake for breakfast, but who wouldn't want a nice carrot muffin? It sounds like health food, even with the layer of cream cheese frosting!

A study in the *Journal of Consumer Research* shows that individuals who are dieting or trying to eat healthy foods have learned to avoid some foods by name. Hence, they will skip a milk shake, but will still order a healthier-sounding smoothie.[6]

In fact, the researchers found that the same dish containing vegetables, pasta, meat, and cheese was rated as healthier when it was called "salad" instead of "pasta." Another test showed that subjects ate more "fruit chews" than "candy chews," even though the product was the same.

Beyond Food

I'm sure that every industry has some examples of transformative naming. Liquid soap was around for years before "shower gel" transformed how we bathe. In some cases, like the food examples, the name is a means to shed a negative image for a product that people enjoy. Potato chips taste great but are loaded with carbs and fat. Veggie chips taste great, have plenty of carbs and fat, but *sound* so much more virtuous! (In each case, product and package adjustments accompanied the renaming.)

Brainfluence Takeaway: Rename Your Category

If your sales are stalled, it may be time to think outside the box—that is, your product's current box! If your product has any negative connotations, or even if some aspect of it, like an ingredient, is problematic, renaming (and changing it a little) could be part of the solution to increasing sales.

This may be difficult. If you are in the candy business, your first thought isn't to label a product as something other than candy or to reformulate and repackage to make the product less candy-like. Nevertheless, some creative reflection may give you a "new" product that is closer to what your customers are looking for. (Creativity is great, but don't get so imaginative that you misrepresent the underlying product!)

Describing your product in a new way may not be all that difficult; after decades of selling "prunes" to aging, constipated people, fruit companies in the United States also offer "dried plums" to a new generation of young, vigorous, health-oriented consumers. Renaming the category on some of their products allowed them to shed the old prune stereotypes at far lower cost than trying to get consumers to reimagine the stodgy prune. Not only did they avoid an expensive image makeover for prunes, they could keep selling the wrinkled fruit to their traditional base with no loss of revenue.

63

Why Percentages Don't Add Up

WHICH WOULD YOU find more frightening: undergoing a potentially fatal surgical procedure that has a 95 percent survival rate or one that causes death in 1 out of 20 patients? If you are like most people, you would find the latter statistic far more worrisome, even though mathematically the two statements are the same. A variety of research shows that marketers should choose carefully when throwing numbers at their customers.

Although Jason Zweig's excellent neuroeconomics book, *Your Money and Your Brain*, is geared to showing how poorly our brains are wired for evaluating investments, it has plenty of content useful to marketers. Zweig spends time discussing framing—how the way information is presented can affect the way it is interpreted. One of the more surprising examples of framing is the difference between percentages and absolute numbers.[7]

Zweig notes that people react differently even to the subtle variation between "10 percent" and "1 out of every 10." For example, he cites an experiment that showed 79 percent of psychiatrists would release a patient who had a 20 percent chance of committing a violent act within six months, but only 59 percent would release a patient when they were told that "20 out of 100" similar patients would commit such an act.

Another experiment showed that people believed cancer to be 32 percent riskier when told that it kills 1,286 out of every 10,000 people, versus 12.86 percent of people.

The difference is that numbers imply *real people*. A 2 percent chance of misfortune sounds low, but if you hear that 2 people out of 100 will be harmed, your brain imagines two actual people suffering an injury.

Brainfluence Takeaway: Use Real Numbers for Impact

If you want to convey a positive message, use real numbers, not percentages. If you are describing a benefit of your product or service, expressing it in terms of absolute numbers will maximize its impact.

Good: 90 percent of our customers rate our service as "excellent"

Better: 9 out of 10 customers rate our service as "excellent"

Present Negative Data as Percentages

If you must present negative information (and are not bound legally to present it in a particular way), expressing it as a percentage may mute its impact somewhat. In general, of course, it's better to focus on the positive; few marketers would include negative information in their ads voluntarily. ("Most people like our product a lot, but 5 percent think it sucks!" is an unlikely tagline.)

Sometimes, when marketers *do* have to include negative information, such as the side effects of a pharmaceutical product, they may have specific legal requirements as to what they can and can't say. But there are times when marketing and public relations people do have to address negative topics, as when dealing with press coverage of a company problem. In these cases, I'd recommend percentages. "Only 1 percent of our laptops have actually caught on fire" is, from a framing standpoint, better than, "Only 1 out of 100 . . ." Bad news is bad news, but people will be less likely to visualize their legs getting scorched if they don't imagine themselves as "the one."

Percentages Still Have Their Uses

A product that is 99.94 percent pure does indeed sound free of contaminants, and there may not be a better way of making the point. In that case, though, the writer isn't expecting the reader to really analyze or understand the number beyond the fact that it is really close to a perfect 100 percent.

In short, to communicate with clarity and impact, use real numbers whenever possible. Your targets will understand you better and identify more closely with the statistics when they relate to numbers of people.

64

Magic Word #1: FREE!

It's NOT BIG news that "FREE!" is a potent word in copy. For decades, that word has been on every list of attention-getting words for copywriters. More recently, Chris Anderson wrote an entire book about the concept of "free" and how it is becoming a consumer expectation.

FREE! is indeed special. Research conducted by author and Duke professor Dan Ariely shows us that "free" is far more effective than "almost free." Indeed, a preference for "free" seems to be another feature hardwired into our brains.

Free Kisses Beat Bargain Truffles

In his book *Predictably Irrational,* Ariely describes a series of simple experiments that offered subjects something desirable—chocolate—at a variety of prices. Two types of chocolate were used: a Hershey's Kiss and a Lindt chocolate truffle. Whereas the Kiss is an inexpensive and rather pedestrian treat, a Lindt truffle is a far tastier confection that costs an order of magnitude more than the Kiss.

The first experiment offered subjects a truffle for 15 cents (about half its actual cost) or a Kiss for 1 cent. Nearly three out of four subjects chose the truffle, which seems logical enough based on the relative value of the offers.

The next experiment reduced the price of each product by one cent—the truffle was offered at 14 cents, and the Kiss was free. Although the price differential remained the same, the behavior of the subjects changed dramatically: more than two thirds of the subjects chose the free chocolate Kiss over the bargain-priced truffle.

To see if the appeal of the free chocolate was based on convenience (not having any change, having to hunt around in a purse for coins, etc.), the experiment was repeated in a cafeteria food line where the cost of the chocolate could be easily added to the total purchase. Even with the elimination of paying inconvenience, the free Kiss was still the overwhelming choice.

Ariely attributes the preference for free even when the rational choice would be the bargain item to our brain's aversion to loss. In essence, a free item carries no risk. Ariely may be right, although I think another explanation is that, to our hunter-gatherer brain, a free item represents the proverbial low-hanging fruit. That is, a resource that can be obtained with near-zero effort. If, millennia before money and commerce came into being, I had just gorged on fruit and had an adequate supply of food stored in my cave, I would be unlikely to go looking for more food. But, if I was walking back to my cave and found a perfect apple hanging over the path in easy reach, I'd no doubt be tempted to pluck it and figure out what to do with it later. That apple would be, in essence, free—other food sources might involve climbing, stalking, traveling, or other kinds of effort.

Amazon's Experience With FREE!

The most interesting example of the power of free in *Predictably Irrational* comes from Amazon.com. When Amazon launched a free shipping promotion with the purchase of a second book, every country except France showed a big jump in sales from the offer. The Amazon marketers investigated, thinking perhaps the French were rational enough not to be swayed into buying a second book.

In fact, they found that in France the program had been slightly altered. Instead of zero shipping, the offer in France charged a mere one franc—about 20 cents. From a pure economic standpoint, the two offers are almost indistinguishable. In actual performance, though, the one franc offer caused no sales increase. (When the French offer was changed to free, sales did indeed jump.)

Brainfluence Takeaway: Tap Into the Power of FREE!

FREE! is more powerful than any rational economic analysis would suggest. If you want to sell more of something, use that power. I often see department store offers such as, "Buy one pair of slacks at regular price, get a second pair for only one penny!" That may sound clever—"Wow, pants for just a penny!"—but I think free will outperform the penny offer. Want to spark sales of a product? Try offering something free with it. Want to get the widest possible sampling of a new product? Use a free sample.

When **Not** to Use FREE!

There are some cases when using FREE! isn't the best idea. If you are trying to encourage sampling of a product that appeals to a specific audience, for example, a very modest charge will throttle demand but will eliminate most samplers who have no use for the product. For example, I don't own a cat. I don't even care much for cats. But if the supermarket had a big display of "Free Cat Food Samples," there's a good chance that I'd pick one up, thinking that I'd give it to a friend. Or maybe I'd hang onto it for when one of the inevitable stray cats shows up. Hey, it's FREE!—I'll grab it now and figure out what to do with it later.

Ariely's research suggests that pricing the cat food sample at, say, a mere 10 cents, would almost certainly slash inappropriate sampling by people like me. A few legitimate cat owners might avoid the sample, too, but the overall cost/benefit of the program would likely improve.

65

Magic Word #2: NEW!

ANOTHER WORD THAT is a perennial entry in every list of attention-getting words for advertising is "NEW!" Neuroscientists have now determined that the appeal of NEW! is hardwired into our brains.

Novelty activates our brain's reward center, which may have been an evolutionary advantage to our ancestors as they encountered new food sources or other elements of survival. Today, we are no longer hunters and gatherers, but the novelty-seeking circuitry is still active and makes us find new products (and even repackaged old products) attractive.

Researcher Bianca Wittmann and her teams had subjects choose cards associated with small rewards while scanning their brains using fMRI. Over time, the subjects were shown cards with which they had become familiar as well as new ones. The researchers found that making novel choices lit up the brain's ventral striatum, an evolutionarily primitive part of the brain and an area associated with rewarding behavior. Wittmann speculates that dopamine, a neurotransmitter that is part of the brain's reward process, is released when a novel choice is made.[8]

Brainfluence Takeaway: Make It NEW!

Make a product "new" in some way, and it will get a boost when compared with competing products. At the same time, marketers should be mindful of long-term brand attachments. (Will Coca-Cola ever forget the New Coke disaster?) For example, changing a brand's logo might provide a short-term novelty boost, but it might also weaken brand familiarity and attachment.

Since we know that brain scans show that familiar brands cause higher levels of brain activation than unfamiliar ones (see page 53), marketers need to steer a careful course. You should emphasize the novelty of your offering while still using the power of long-term brand affinity.

66

Adjectives That Work

COMPELLING, EMOTION-RICH adjectives can give bland copy a major boost in effectiveness. (Just like the start of that sentence!) I was reminded of this while viewing a Panera menu. Which do you think sounds more appealing:

Ham, egg, & cheese on wheat bread sandwich.

or

Our Breakfast Power Sandwich starts with lean, hardwood-smoked ham and a freshly-cracked egg. Then we add Vermont white cheddar for its tangy sharpness. Finally, we grill everything on our freshly baked whole grain bread to bring out the grains' nutty, smooth flavors.

Take a look at the adjectives that turn an average sandwich into a mouthwatering, tantalizing sales magnet:

Our **Breakfast Power** Sandwich starts with **lean, hardwood-smoked** ham and a **freshly-cracked** egg. Then we add **Vermont white cheddar** [cheese] for its **tangy** sharpness. Finally, we grill everything on our **freshly-baked whole grain** bread to bring out the grains' **nutty, smooth** flavors.

If people aren't lining up to buy this sandwich, it's not the copywriter's fault. (Sadly for Panera, though, most patrons see only the minimalist description on the in-restaurant menu board.)

Adjectives aren't without controversy. Some copy experts think adjectives slow down the reader and reduce comprehension. But research shows that properly used adjectives actually *increase* revenue.

For example, Dr. Brian Wansink studied the effect of descriptive menu labels and found they increased sales by as much as 27 percent. He divided his adjectives into categories, including geographic (e.g., "Southwestern Tex-Mex salad") and sensory (e.g., "buttery plump pasta"). Branding adjectives can help too, like "Jack Daniels" barbecue sauce.

According to Wansink, not only do vivid descriptors nudge patrons toward a purchase, they also increase satisfaction at the end of the meal compared with the same food without the labeling.[9]

Although we can likely all agree that "applewood-smoked bacon" is more enticing than plain old "bacon," most of us don't run restaurants. Still, we can learn from what those food establishments have found to be effective. When it makes sense, enhance the impact of your descriptive copy with carefully chosen adjectives. I'll offer my own variation on Wansink's categories of modifiers:

Vivid—"Freshly-cracked" is much more compelling than "fresh."

Sensory—Terms such as "hickory-smoked," "brick oven–fired," and "oven-crisped," engage the reader's senses.

Emotional/nostalgic—"Aged Vermont cheddar" evokes images of crusty New England dairymen rather than Kraft megaplants.

Specific—"Wild Alaskan" attached to a salmon description immediately enhances it with visions of vigorous, healthy fish swimming in pristine, unpolluted streams.

Branded—Attaching desirable brand names to a description can boost sales. I'm sure it hasn't been cheap for restaurants to offer "Jack Daniels" barbecue items, but their continued menu presence suggests branding with the famous whiskey name more than pays for itself.

These adjectives are processed unconsciously most of the time. Do you really ponder whether the tomato on your burger is "farm-fresh" as the menu claims? What does "farm-fresh" mean, anyway? Do some restaurants use tomatoes that don't come from farms or that are spoiled? (More likely, the tomatoes are so fresh that they started green, had to be ethylene-ripened and are still as hard as croquet balls!)

While your conscious mind is thinking about the price, how much cash is in your wallet, and whether the item will blow your diet, those sensory and emotional terms are being processed in the background.

Brainfluence Takeaway: Season Your Copy With Vivid Adjectives

Your own challenge is to find the adjectives that work for your product or service. What emotions do you want to evoke in your customers? A feeling of, say, tradition and craftsmanship? cutting-edge technology? personal service? Find relevant, compelling adjectives, and your copy will be more effective.

Striking a Balance

In your quest to liven up your copy, don't go overboard. As enticing as the Panera sandwich description is, most of us would hate to read more than a few lines written in that style.

Your message is told mainly by nouns and verbs, and too many adjectives slow down the reader and muddle your message. That's particularly true if they are boring words that add little in the way of sensory or emotional engagement.

Just like adding too much Hawaiian Red and Black Sea Salt (yes, it exists) to your recipe, it's certainly possible to overdo things even with vivid and enticing modifiers. Use adjectives in short product descriptions and similar places, but leave them out of your call to action, your ordering instructions, and anywhere else where quick, easy comprehension is critical.

67

Your Brain on Stories

"They laughed when I sat down at the piano . . ."

"On a beautiful late spring afternoon, twenty-five years ago, two young men graduated from the same college. They were very much alike, these two young men. Both had been better than average students . . ."

ADVERTISING BUFFS INSTANTLY recognize these two opening lines. The first is from an ad penned by the legendary John Caples promoting music lessons by mail. The second is the beginning of a Martin Conroy–written *Wall Street Journal* ad, which Brian Clark, principal author of the popular *Copyblogger* website, describes as "the greatest sales letter of all time."

What do these two ads have in common, besides being amazingly successful and nearly ageless? (Both campaigns ran for decades essentially unchanged, unheard of in the fast-changing world of advertising.) The answer is simple: these unusually effective ads each *tell a story*.

Why Stories Engage Our Brain

Evolutionary psychologists think our brains' affinity for stories is hardwired and that it provided early humans a significant advantage over other species. While most animals learn by experience—"the red bumpy fruit makes you sick," for example—humans can describe their experiences and other humans can imagine them as if they were experiencing the same thing.

There's modern-day proof that stories allow vivid sharing of experiences. Scientists put subjects in an fMRI machine while they read an exciting passage from a Hardy Boys novel. The scans showed that the subjects' brains lit up in different places for different passages. For example, when the story characters were grabbing objects, motor neurons were activated; vision-related neurons fired up when the characters were observing their environment.[10]

Psychology writer Herbert Wray thinks we aren't passive when we read but, rather, our brains turn on "scripts" based on real-world experiences. Because of this, Wray says that "reading is much like remembering or imagining a vivid event."

The Mind-Meld Effect

Princeton researchers monitored brain activity in pairs of subjects while one told the other a story. They found that when the subjects communicated, neural activity in their brains became almost synchronous. A second after specific brain activity was observed in the speaker's brain, this same pattern was repeated in the listener's brain.[11]

The brain scans show that such neural coupling doesn't always occur—it happened only when the listener was paying attention and understood the story.

Advertising Stories

Clearly, the narratives in the successful ads resonated in some special and universal way with their readers. We've all experienced moments of social discomfort, much like the would-be pianist who sits down at the piano only to have his friends laugh. And we've all had moments of pride when others acknowledge our skill or accomplishments.

The narrative nature of the wording in "They laughed when I sat down . . ." brings these deep-seated memories to the surface to produce a more profound effect than had the ad copy simply suggested that we could impress our friends if we could play the piano.

Brainfluence Takeaway: Tell a Vivid Story

To engage potential customers, write a vivid story involving your product or brand. Include action, motion, dialogue, and other aspects that will activate different parts of your customers' brains. This approach has worked for the best copywriters and most successful ads in history, and it can work for you.

68

Use Story Testimonials

WE KNOW THAT anecdotes can be a convincing way to sell a product, particularly if someone we trust tells the story. This harks back to a time when our brains were evolving and humans had two ways to learn about dangers and rewards in their environment: personal experience and communication from other trusted humans.

Trusted stories are still important, even when our personal networks are far-flung and so much communication is electronic. For most of us, an average rating of 3.7 stars for a nearby restaurant is far less powerful than a description of a friend's nightmarish experience on her last visit to the establishment.

As Christopher Chabris and Daniel Simons point out in *The Invisible Gorilla:*[12]

We naturally generalize from one example to the population as a whole, and our memories for such inferences are inherently sticky. Individual examples lodge in our minds, but statistics and averages do not . . . Our ancestors lacked access to huge data sets, statistics, and experimental methods. By necessity, we learned from specific examples, not by compiling data from many people across a wide range of situations.

Statistics are simply less interesting and relevant to our brains than detailed anecdotes. This is why successful infomercials always include personal success stories told by the individuals themselves. (Another reason might be that they lack the statistically valid research to back up their claims!) Even if you can show that two thirds of the people who used your diet aid lost weight, having one credible individual tell her personal story can be much more potent.

These infomercial stories usually provide plenty of detail—the individual's situation before using the product, how that person felt, what the first experience with the product was like, and so on. This detail all plays to our brain's ability to silently simulate what it is hearing.

Sadly, even bogus stories exercise considerable influence. In the United States, childhood diseases that had been nearly nonexistent are making a comeback due to scientifically unfounded fears that vaccines cause autism. A raft of statistics demonstrating the safety of the vaccines, and even pronouncements by groups of eminent scientists, proved to be less powerful than the stories of mothers of autistic children who attributed the condition to a vaccine injection. Scientists can dismiss such claims as anecdotal and produce statistics that show no cause and effect, but the unfortunate truth is that our brains respond to anecdotes.

Brainfluence Takeaway: Go Beyond Short Testimonials

Short testimonials are not a bad thing at all. Letting potential customers know that other real people used your product with success is always a good thing and constitutes social proof. But don't stop there. Turning a testimonial into a personal anecdote will greatly increase its impact. Adding a name, a face, and a story will play to the way our brains evolved and be more convincing and more memorable.

Our brain's preference for trusted stories explains why word of mouth is such a powerful tool: if the story is told by someone we actually know, not by a celebrity or paid endorser, it will be even more credible and potent.

69

When Words Are Worth a Thousand Pictures

WHAT MAKES AN engaging television commercial? If you think visual and auditory appeal—action, sound, music, people, color, and so on—you would usually be correct. Ditto for high production values. An exotic location might help too. All of these capabilities explain why advertisers love the video medium, particularly for creating an emotional reaction in the viewer.

For years, copywriters have had to suffer under the maxim that "a picture is worth a thousand words." (Just imagine how many words a video would be worth!) But, a recent Super Bowl provided an example that should warm the hearts of copywriters everywhere: Google's entry into the big league of Super Bowl advertising with their "Parisian Love" ad.[13]

This ad is quite different from the typical Super Bowl commercial, and, indeed, from almost any television spot that you have seen. There are no dogs, horses, or monkeys. No scenery. No fast cars. No gorgeous women. In fact there are no humans at all. Other than a few small, fleetingly seen maps, the only graphic element is the prominent Google logo.

What the ad *does* have is *text* . . . lots of text. Not only does the ad have text to read, but there's plenty of spurious text that the viewer has to ignore while trying to keep up with the rapidly changing screens. Just as in real Google searches, multiple suggestions are shown, as are multiple results for each completed search. Despite the quick screen changes and irrelevant content, though, viewers can easily follow the story spelled out by the searches.

So, to recap so far . . . Google decided to spend nearly $3 million to air an ad that cost next to nothing to produce, has no actors or computer-generated images (CGI) or animation, no cute animals—nothing but a series of words typed into search boxes and the generated search results. At first glance, this might sound like E-Trade's famous, "We just wasted $2 million bucks" ad, but it's not.

In fact, this unlikely ad was highly effective.

How do we know? One indicator might be critical acclaim. Every year, marketing professors at Michigan State University rank the Super Bowl ads, and in 2010, their top choice of the 60 commercials was Google's ad. Their reasoning was that it had a "fantastic story, low production costs and the surprise factor. It sells what they do in a simple way."[14]

A more telling indicator, though, might be how people responded physically and emotionally to the ad. Neuromarketing company Sands Research conducted a study of all 60 or so ads that aired during the 2010 Super Bowl, and Google's Parisian Love ad came in fourth in terms of what Sands calls "neuro-engagement."[15]

That an ad consisting entirely of text could outscore nearly all of the high-budget, high-production value Super Bowl ads was a surprise, according to the firm's founder Stephen Sands. He commented that in addition to the high neuro-engagement score, the Google ad was one of the most-remembered ads when the subjects were surveyed after the experiment.

**Brainfluence Takeaway: Text Beats Richer Media
When It Tells a Story**

Even in a highly visual medium like television, properly used text can beat commercials with amazing imagery, sound, and production values. From a branding and memorability standpoint, having a giant Google logo on the screen much of the time is likely a good thing, but the key to the ad's engagement was its compelling plot. This Google commercial is further proof that text can be amazingly powerful when it tells a story.

70

The Million-Dollar Pickle

YEARS AGO, I listened to a keynote speech focused on customer service. The speaker's centerpiece was "the pickle story." Briefly, this guy discovered he was out of pickles just before a big Sunday cookout at his house and made an emergency run to the closest supermarket. He arrived home with the pickles and opened the jar, only to find that the top pickle appeared to have a large bite out of it. His wife confirmed the diagnosis, so he rushed back to the store again. That's when things headed south.

He was met by surliness and indifference by the store's staff. The clerk eyed him with suspicion, and two managers were called over. They conferred, examining the pickle in question and glancing repeatedly at their customer. Clearly, they had decided that if anyone took a bite out of that pickle, it was the joker who now wanted a different jar. Although the store eventually replaced the bottle, the combination of terrible attitude and lengthy delay made our speaker vow never to shop at the store again.

He also vowed to spread the word far and wide. He told his guests at the cookout. He told his neighbors. He told the audiences he spoke to. I won't attempt to duplicate the math, but he calculated that the hassle over a $1.50 jar of pickles cost the store thousands of dollars in purchases that he and his family would have made in the following years. He estimated the store's losses at an amount in the millions of dollars if even a portion of the people who heard his pickle story decided to try shopping someplace else.

Did that speaker cost the store millions in lost sales? Who knows? But there's little doubt the story lodged in the brains of those who listened to it. I didn't even know the guy, and I still remember the story many years later. I'm sure he had lots of great information about how good companies take care of their customers and had impressive statistics that demonstrate the effects of good service. But what's the *only* thing I remember? The pickle story!

Most likely, I would have remembered the name of the supermarket chain, too, but it wasn't one that served my area; I'm sure many of those who heard the story firsthand *did* remember the name and stored it as an essential part of that story.

Brainfluence Takeaway: Don't Create Negative Stories

We know that stories can sell in part because they make our brains light up in sympathy with what we are hearing and that anecdotes are more powerful than statistics. The pickle story is a great example of a story that will hurt sales, and will persist in the minds of those who hear it. Stories like that can affect the perception of the unfortunate merchant for years to come.

The persistence of the story in my own memory, despite not recall-ing the speaker's name, the venue, the name of the event, or any other details, illustrates how sticky stories can be.

You can't make people forget a memorable tale of poor service or problematic products, so your best defense is to speedily resolve every problem before it turns into your own "million-dollar pickle" story.

SECTION

Ten

Consumer Brainfluence

NEUROSCIENCE AND BEHAVIOR research have provided many, many insights into how consumers make decisions. Here are some of the best and most actionable!

This has ended up being a catchall category for neuromarketing techniques that may not fit neatly into a single medium but that can be applied in multiple ways.

71

Simple Marketing for Complex Products

THE MORE COMPLEX a decision is, the more thought and deliberation it requires, right? As intuitive and seemingly obvious as that statement seems, research shows that it's not true, at least in some kinds of situations. A study at the University of Amsterdam on how we make decisions led to a surprising conclusion: simple decisions seem to work out best when made with more thought, whereas complex decisions seem better when made intuitively.[1]

One experiment had subjects assess the quality of four hypothetical automobiles using either 4 or 12 attributes. Those who were given four attributes chose the better-quality cars more accurately when they were allowed to think about it, whereas subjects who were distracted (and who couldn't deliberate) made worse choices. Surprisingly, though, the results were reversed for the subjects who had more information (12 attributes): the distracted subjects actually made better choices than the subjects who were allowed to concentrate on the decision.

Of greater marketing interest, perhaps, is another experiment by the same group that measured the satisfaction of subjects with purchase decisions they made. The researchers surveyed shoppers leaving two stores, De Bijenkorf, which sells clothes, a simple product, and IKEA, a seller of complex products like furniture. (I suspect the researchers who found clothing to be a simple product were mostly male!)

The researchers found that the purchasers of simple products were happiest with their decision when they had thought long and hard about the purchase, whereas the reverse was true for those who bought more complex products. The happiest buyers for the complex products were those who decided with little conscious deliberation.[2]

The study concluded that decision makers leave more complex decisions to the subconscious. I'm not sure I completely buy into this strategy. Sometimes, complex products actually require detailed analysis to make a good decision. Periodically, I evaluate smartphones, for example—a complex product if there ever was one. Each phone has dozens of important variables: screen size, keyboard type and layout, overall weight, battery life under different conditions, data connection speed, service availability in different geographic areas, operating system, available data plans, and many others.

The models are usually quite different in many respects, and a unit that excels in one area may be deficient in another. This is truly a complex problem, but careful analysis *is* important; buying an expensive phone that proves to be incompatible with my scheduling software, has a difficult-to-use keyboard, or has limited broadband service in a geographic area I frequent is a prescription for disaster.

On the other hand, we've all had times when we've devoted way too much thought to buying an item. I've noticed that doing lots of research may promote buyer's remorse; even when you make the best choice, you are still aware of the flaws of the thing you bought and of those areas where a competing item excels.

Brainfluence Takeaway: Give Buyers a Simple Reason to Buy Your Complex Product

If we accept the idea that some complex decisions are best made without lots of deliberation, how should that affect our marketing? It's a matter of degree. If you are selling a complex product like an automobile, give the customer a simple reason to buy your product. Make the specifications and features available to the consumer, because people like me will want to analyze the details; however, don't lead with six new features or 10 reasons to buy the product.

A simple message, like "#1 in customer satisfaction" or "more safety features than any car in its class" will go farther in steering the consumer down the intuitive decision path. After all, if the car I'm buying is #1 in customer satisfaction, do I really need to sweat the details? Maybe not. An even simpler approach is a nonverbal emotional appeal, such as showing the car in a setting that exudes wealth, glamour, and luxury.

Simple marketing messages have always been appealing for their clarity and memorability. The flip side of the research, though, is that very simple products, such as toothpaste and socks, may do better with more information. Indeed, scanning the toothpaste aisle today reveals products with an almost bewildering array of features. Toothpaste is no longer a simple commodity for dental cleaning; now, products offer various combinations of whitening, tartar control, cavity prevention, breath freshening, gum care, and other features. Consumers can zero in on their oral hygiene priorities and find a product that's a perfect match.

One caution: even though the research shows that consumers *should* make decisions in this manner for best results (in terms of both decision quality and their own satisfaction), it doesn't mean that people *will* decide this way. The researchers found no shortage of shoppers who bought simple products impulsively and complex products with a lot of thought. Even if these strategies weren't optimal, that's how those consumers made their choices.

At best, a marketing campaign can guide the customer toward one strategy or the other, but it can't force a customer to decide in a way that he or she doesn't want to. So allow for different types of decision makers, whether the product is simple or complicated.

72

Sell to the Inner Infovore

ALTHOUGH THE TERM *infovore* has been kicking around for a while as a cute name for a consumer of information, the University of Southern California's Irving Biederman uses the term to describe humans exhibiting a more specific kind of behavior: an innate desire for information and learning. Biederman's work shows there is a feedback mechanism in the brain that rewards the acquisition of knowledge and that most humans have a "knowledge addiction."[3]

Biederman thinks we are programmed to be information junkies. From an evolutionary standpoint, perceived intelligence is a key factor in mate selection, he notes. Biederman even attributes our appreciation for art to the same quest for new information.

In coming up with this theory, Biederman linked pleasure receptors in the brain to the way we process new visual stimuli. Seeing something new increases activity in that area of the brain, and the reward system kicks in.

According to Biederman, we unconsciously seek things that are rich in information and novel. Although his work focused on the processing of visual information, he speculates that similar findings would apply to other senses.

Brainfluence Takeaway: Show 'Em Something New

What can marketers derive from Biederman's research? Perhaps the most important finding is that people experience a neurochemical reward when they acquire new information. That information doesn't have to be reading *War and Peace* or learning the proof for a mathematical theorem; it could be as simple as seeing a new, unfamiliar picture.

So, although conventional advertising wisdom suggests that repetition is an essential part of changing customer behavior, Biederman's work shows that the brain tends to tune out familiar images in favor of novel ones. Hence, advertisers must strike a balance between repeating their message but also providing novel information to trigger the reward circuits in the brain.

Market Like Absolut

One successful ad campaign that is an excellent example of infovore marketing is Absolut Vodka's long-running print campaign of bottle-shaped images. Long before neuromarketing was conceived, Absolut's ad people devised a campaign that provided intriguing, novel images incorporating the distinctive shape of the Absolut bottle. These highly creative images not only were original but often contained a bit of humor or playfully incorporated some concept that would take a bit of thought for the viewer to fully connect.

From an infovore perspective, one would have to say these images were just about perfect. Not only were they novel and unexpected, they produced a little "aha, I get it!" reward to the viewer who decoded the image.

73

Want Versus Should: Time Your Pitch

EVERYONE IS FAMILIAR with the *want* versus *should* conflict. Do you order the loaded cheese fries as your side dish or the steamed broccoli? You *want* the greasy fries, but you know you *should* order the broccoli. Do you mow the grass (should) or watch football (want)?

Harvard researchers Todd Rogers and Katherine Milkman think two personalities reside in all of us: the want-self and the should-self. Table 73.1 shows some typical behavioral conflict.

Timing Is Critical

The study showed that timing was critical in the want versus should battle. A decision on food for immediate consumption favored want items. Purchases for consumption days in the future were more likely to be healthy and nutritious (should items).[4,5]

Table 73.1 *Want* Versus *Should*

Want-self	Should-self
Short-term gratification	Long-term benefit
Junk food	Healthy food
Spend now	Save for later
Watch television	Exercise

Movie Battles

Food isn't the only battleground between our want-self and should-self where time of consumption differences exist. The same researchers studied DVD rental patterns and found that people ordered documentary (*should* watch) DVDs before action and other entertainment films (*want* to watch). They tended to return the documentaries after the other DVDs, however, indicating that at the moment of consumption (putting the DVD in the player), the want-self won out over the should-self.

Brainfluence Takeaway: Time Your Pitch to *Wants* and *Shoulds*

The implications of this work are significant for many kinds of marketers. Just about every marketer sells either want or should items, and many sell both.

Sell Want Items for Immediate Use

Based on these studies, sales of want items can be maximized when they will be used right away; should items do best if marketed for future use. The authors point out that fruits and vegetables are among the first things the consumers sees as they begin to push their carts around the grocery store; this makes sense, as the beginning of the shopping trip is farthest away from time of product use.

I assume the same logic dictates why the supermarkets place candy bars right at the checkout. These items may not even make it to the car before they are consumed!

Selling Online

The authors comment that online sellers and catalog merchants should be sure to take delivery time into account when promoting their merchandise. Consumers are likely to order more want items if they are available for immediate delivery. On the other hand, they caution that customers will spend less overall the further in advance of delivery the order is placed.

Everything Else

These lessons could apply to just about anything. Selling sports cars? Assure the customer that he can drive away in his new convertible as soon as he signs the papers. Selling vitamins? Offer a promotion favoring purchases of a six-month supply, maybe even with a delayed payment and periodic shipments.

First, determine whether you are selling a want or a should; then, choose an appropriate timing strategy. As with many things in life and business, in the battle between the customer's want-self and should-self, timing is everything.

74

Sell to Tightwads

A QUARTER OF your potential customers may be particularly challenging to sell to. They are classified as tightwads, individuals who are particularly reluctant to part with their money.

Research at Carnegie Mellon University showed that some individuals feel so much buying pain that they tend to avoid spending money—even in situations where most individuals would find the expense to be justified and of good value; these are tightwads. Spendthrifts, meanwhile, seem to feel little buying pain and spend money even in situations where most individuals would avoid doing so.[6]

According to the researchers, the differences in behavior between the two groups are strongest in scenarios where the pain of paying is maximized (e.g., immediate payment in full) and smallest in situations with the least buying pain (e.g., payment deferred into the future). They also find a distinction between tightwads and people who are frugal. Frugal people don't feel more buying pain than the rest of us; they simply enjoy saving. That distinction may be inconsequential in some situations, but it's important to note that the underlying motivation of frugality is different.

A survey of more than 13,000 individuals showed the following breakdown:

Tightwads—24 percent

Unconflicted—60 percent

Spendthrifts—15 percent

Some marketers may be disappointed that free spenders comprise only 15 percent of their potential customer base, but the key takeaway is that there are major portions of the population who are wired to respond to marketing offers in quite different ways. Ignoring these differences may result in an underperforming ad campaign or sales effort.

One of the defining questions in the survey was how much credit card debt the subject had. Spendthrifts were three times as likely as tightwads to have credit card debt. Perhaps unsurprisingly, tightwads reported higher levels of personal savings than spendthrifts.

Brainfluence Takeaway: Minimize the Pain for Tightwads (and Everyone Else)

Although an in-person sales effort can adjust to customer characteristics on the fly, print and other media campaigns may have to come up with an approach that is geared to the most likely buyer groups or develop somewhat different campaigns if it makes sense to try to target all groups of customers.

The overall approach that seems likely to work across the board is to minimize buying pain in a given offer.

1. *Make the price a bargain.* Tightwads don't like high prices, or prices that appear to be high for what they are buying. Sale prices are more potent tools with this group. In a direct selling situation where the offer can be tailored to the individual, a price discount can help seal the deal. In most selling situations, though, discounting may not be a desirable option, or even a possibility. In these cases, try restating the price in different terms. An annual membership costing $120 might be described as "only $10 per month" or "only 33 cents per day." In every case, you are trying to show the tightwad buyer how fair the price is for the value received.

2. *Avoid repeated pain points.* Per-item pricing (as in a sushi restaurant) creates a more painful buying situation than a one-time, all-inclusive price (as in a seafood buffet). Since tightwads are more sensitive to paying pain, avoid "drip-drip-drip" pricing structures that punish the buyer every time she does something. Obviously, not all selling situations allow this. Walmart can't adopt "per-cart" or "all-you-can-buy" pricing. But many products and services, including Internet service, cell phone service plans, health club memberships, and physical products with options, are possibilities for converting à la carte items in a package price.

3. *Create product bundles.* This is closely related to the previous point. One effect of package pricing is to disguise individual pain points, as has been noted by neuroeconomics expert George Loewenstein. One example he cites is the bundling of car accessories, such as leather seats, power features, and so on, into a single "luxury package." This avoids the multiple pain points of selecting separately priced items and also disguises the individual prices. If the packaged items were sold individually, the consumer would have to make a specific decision on whether leather seats were worth an extra $1,000, a power moonroof, $900 more, and so on. Even though the package may cost as much as, or even more

than, the individual components priced separately, there's less buying pain involved.

One good thing: if you can reduce the buying pain associated with your offer, you'll almost certainly do better with the vast majority of your potential customers. All but the most extreme spendthrifts do feel some buying pain, and a less painful offer will help with more than tightwad customers.

4. *Appeal to important needs.* Tightwads are less likely to be seduced by the sex appeal of a product than other types of buyers. One of the experiments conducted by the CMU researchers was to present an offer of a $100 massage couched either in utilitarian terms (relief of back pain) or hedonic terms (a pleasurable experience). Although tightwads were 26 percent less likely to buy the hedonic massage than the spendthrifts, they lagged by only 9 percent for the utilitarian massage. Most products combine a variety of characteristics, and the utilitarian ones may be most important to emphasize when selling to tightwads.

5. *Watch your language!* One rather startling finding in the CMU research was that changing the description of an overnight shipping charge on a free DVD offer from a "$5 fee" to a "small $5 fee" increased the response rate among tightwads by 20 percent! This is hardly inventive copywriting, but the mere reminder that $5 was a small amount of money had an important effect on tightwads.

In short, don't write off a big chunk of your potential customers as too cheap to bother marketing to. Instead, refine your approach to your tightwad customers, and you'll steal market share from your less aware competitors and boost sales across the board.

75

Sell to Spendthrifts

NEUROECONOMICS RESEARCH SHOWS that roughly 15 percent of your consumers are spendthrifts—people who have unusually low sensitivity to the pain of paying, that is, the neural discomfort associated with parting with money.

Selling to people who feel little or no buying pain should be easy, right? With reduced buying inhibition, a spendthrift is more likely to take advantage of any given offer compared with a tightwad or even a normal, nonconflicted person. Nevertheless, making the sale isn't a given. For one, you have competition; your offer is competing with other offers for similar products or services, as well as offers for dozens of other, unrelated items.

Unless your spendthrift has the net worth of Warren Buffett (who would no doubt qualify as a tightwad), choices will have to be made—as much as the spendthrift might like to, buying everything isn't an option.

Why Worry about Spendthrifts?

If less than one out of six customers falls into the spendthrift category, and they are relatively easy to sell to, why worry about them as a group? I think it's worth thinking about spendthrifts because it is likely that certain types of goods—luxury items, expensive vacations, and the like—are purchased disproportionately by this group.

Is a tightwad likely to buy an expensive Coach purse or Hermes tie? Probably not, unless that tightwad has so much actual wealth that there's little pain associated with buying those items. Marketers of luxury items, not to mention products that are nonessential or even frivolous, should pay particular attention to spendthrift psychology.

Brainfluence Takeaway: Push the Free-Spending Hot Buttons

1. *Appeal to* both *hedonistic and utilitarian tendencies*. Unlike tightwads, spendthrifts are concerned both about utilitarian issues as well as how the product or service will make them feel.

In the previous chapter, we mentioned study of a $100 massage offer that was presented to subjects in two different ways: for some, as a relief from back pain, and for others, as a pleasurable experience. Spendthrifts were much more likely to buy than tightwads when the offer was couched in terms of the massage being a pleasurable experience. Almost half of the spendthrifts bought a pleasurable massage, compared with only about 22 percent of the tightwads. That's more than 100 percent higher.

Interestingly, though, spendthrifts were more likely to buy the therapeutic massage, too—almost 80 percent of the spendthrifts bought the massage, versus a little less than 70 percent of the tightwads. This shows that the most effective offer by far for the spendthrifts was the utilitarian service, but they were also much more responsive to the idea of a pleasurable experience.

What's a marketer to do? If possible, hit *both* hot buttons—you *need* this product, but it's *fun* too. A good example of this kind of marketing is the luxury pickup truck market. A buyer may need the pickup truck for contracting work but also want it to look good and be fun to drive too. (A tightwad corporate buyer, who won't be driving the vehicle personally anyway, might choose an anonymous-looking utility van for the same application.)

2. *Provide and emphasize credit options*. The tightwad study shows that spendthrifts are the most likely group to have credit card debt. Because this group has an above-average willingness to use credit cards,

providing both credit card options as well as other easy financing will help close the deal. Although financing options can help in selling to tightwads too, the reason is different. For tightwads, financing defers and spreads out the buying pain; for spendthrifts, financing options are more important in their role of simply enabling the purchase.

3. *Don't sweat the language.* Although framing a $5 shipping fee as a "small $5 fee" was highly effective in selling to tightwads, it had little effect on spendthrifts. This doesn't mean that wordsmithing should go out the window entirely, but rather that spending a lot of effort to put the pricing in the most favorable light won't help much. Focus on making the product or service appealing to this group.

4. *Offer instant gratification.* Although this was not a conclusion of the Carnegie Mellon University study, I think the behavioral characteristics of spendthrifts suggest that they will be more susceptible to offers that afford either instant or quick gratification.

What's better than a sexy sports car? One you can drive off the lot right now and in minutes be showing off in your driveway or taking for a spin in the country.

5. *Improve margins with options.* Spendthrifts have less sensitivity to buying pain, so some selling situations might use an attractive initial offer to get the buyer to commit and then improve margins with desirable options. The net effect on the package price might be no different than an all-inclusive or bundled offer, but the closure rate might improve.

Are spendthrifts more likely to buy an extended warranty? We have no data on that, but it is likely that in making the trade-off between peace of mind (knowing that whatever goes wrong with your purchase, you'll be covered) and a hefty fee (often 10 percent or more of the purchase price), a spendthrift is more likely to take the offered warranty. Indeed, the reason electronics store clerks are trained to ask every customer about adding the warranty (not unlike the automatic fast-food queries, "fries with that?" and "supersize it?") is that 15 percent of the customer base is wired to be more receptive to that pitch.

76

Take a Chance on a Contest

OUR BRAINS ARE programmed for reward anticipation, but they aren't very good at calculating odds. A Stanford University study shows that big potential rewards produce big responses, even if they are unlikely outcomes. In other words, our brain is very responsive to the *size* of the reward and far less sensitive to the *probability* of actually receiving that reward.[7]

People who stand in line to buy a Powerball ticket when a record jackpot is in play aren't calculating the odds. Even if a statistician was at the ticket dispenser to tell people their odds are much worse than if they wait a week or two, they will ignore that information. If anything, the mobs buying tickets are a form of social proof, not an indication of rapidly declining odds. It's the amount that engages people, not the hard-to-visualize probability of winning.

The analytical part of your brain never has a chance to compete with the reward center lighting up from the prospect of winning a sum bigger than the gross national product of some nations. This human inclination has implications for marketers who use contests, sweepstakes, or other prize offerings. The clear message is that it's the magnitude of the grand prize that is the most important factor in a giveaway. The rest of the details are just that, details.

Golf Lessons

Conventional wisdom at the blackjack table is to decline the insurance offered by the dealer, but for marketers insurance makes sense when it allows a bigger prize. A perfect example is the common "million-dollar hole-in-one" fund-raiser. Golfers make a donation to enter the contest for a chance at winning a million dollars by shooting a hole in one.

There are various rules to reduce the probability of the million dollars actually being paid. The most significant is that the winning shot usually can't take place in the qualifying round when hundreds of golfers may be whacking multiple balls at the cup; the money shot takes place in a final session, when just one or a few golfers (who placed closest to the hole in the first round to qualify) get a chance.

The other technique that eliminates any risk to the charity (a good thing, since one lucky shot might turn a fund-raiser into a financial disaster) is that they can buy insurance. By paying a tiny fixed sum to a firm that offers such coverage (and who ensures the rules of the game minimize the probability of a payout), the charity can offer the million-dollar prize with no fear of catastrophic loss.

The reason those fund-raisers attract entrants is the magnitude of the potential payout. (A desire to support the charity and the justification for playing hooky from the office are no doubt also factors.) The cost of hole-in-one insurance for a million dollars might be as little as a few hundred dollars, but the prize looks enormous.

From the standpoint of a totally rational individual competitor, awarding a few $1,000 prizes to those closest to the hole would have a higher expected payout than the opportunity to qualify for a million-dollar shot. But would logical improvement in the payout generate any excitement? Likely none at all. In short, awarding five $1,000 prizes would cost the charity a lot more than hole-in-one insurance for a million-dollar prize and would almost certainly result in fewer entrants (unless the fund-raiser is targeting mathematicians and statisticians) and a lot less excitement.

Pepsi's Billion Dollars

One company that saw how attractive a big prize could be is soft drink giant Pepsi-Cola. They ran a sweepstakes with a top prize of $1 billion, certainly one of the biggest prizes ever. Like the organizers of your local charity hole-in-one contest, Pepsi took a variety of precautions to avoid financial disaster. They structured the contest as a play-off event, in which first-round winners qualified to continue in a second round and only one contestant ultimately had a chance to match a six-digit number (chosen by a chimpanzee rolling dice!) to win the billion dollars. They also insured the prize via Berkshire Hathaway, the financial powerhouse founded by Warren Buffett. In the unlikely event that the billion-dollar prize had to be awarded, Pepsi wouldn't take a huge hit to the bottom line.[8]

The hoopla surrounding the contest included reality-TV show coverage of the final stages. Of course, the final contestant didn't win the billion dollars. He did walk away with a million, though, and Pepsi garnered a publicity windfall.

Brainfluence Takeaway: Keep Your Eye on the Prize

Business contests have different motivation than charity fund-raisers, but the same principles apply—a spectacular prize is better, even if the odds are low. (One exception may be very-high-frequency prizes, such as those in some fast-food restaurant promotions; in these, there is a high concentration of winning game pieces with small food awards, like free french fries. That's nearly Pavlovian in design!)

When choosing a topline prize, think *big*—even if the odds are lower, people will respond better if there are more zeros at the end of the number. Here are a few ways to maximize the prize value:

- Concentrate the prize budget on one prize.
- Use a play-off system or other approach to permit a huge prize with tightly controlled probability of awarding it.
- Participate in a joint promotion with other companies to increase the prize budget.

(In the United States and other jurisdictions, there are laws that govern contests, so be sure to comply with any relevant legal requirements.)

77

Unconventional Personalization

DALE CARNEGIE ONCE said, "Remember that a man's name is to him the sweetest and most important sound in the English language." It's a good bet that even Carnegie would be surprised at how true that statement is, even at the unconscious level.

Let's start with a quick experiment. Take the first letter of your first name. Now, do you like that letter? Although you might say it's just a letter and you don't like or dislike it, research across many cultures has shown that people like their "initial" letters better than other letters. This preference can be overt, but it also has some strange and unexpected effects on our behavior.

One study showed that students whose names began with A and B got better grades (and were more likely to attend an elite law school) than those whose names began with C and D.[9] The weirdness doesn't stop there. Other research shows that people are more likely to live in cities that resemble their names and choose careers that do the same.[10]

The concept is called implicit egotism. People are generally positive about themselves and tend to be favorable toward things connected to them. Hence, the researchers found that people named Louis are statistically more common in St. Louis, and that people named Dennis and Denise are more frequently dentists than one might predict. Even "birthday numbers" correlated with locations, for example, people born on the third living in Three Rivers.

Other research has shown related effects, including the ownership effect, a preference for an item that one owns over one that belongs to someone else. One study showed that people had a more favorable impression of Rasputin, the "mad monk," when they thought he shared their birthday.[11]

This research is weirdly fascinating. I'm sure lawyers named Lawrence would argue that their name had absolutely nothing to do with their career choice. But what can Marv and Mark, who chose the field of marketing, do with this information?

Brainfluence Takeaway: Try Going Beyond Simple Personalization

Direct marketers know that personalized mailers or e-mails almost always outperform generic versions. But how do they use implicit egotism to further enhance their offerings? Here are a few thoughts.

List Segmentation

Direct marketers still mail catalogs and other marketing pitches, despite the ever-increasing cost of doing so. Mailing lists can be rented and enhanced. For example, a mailer might take a large list of magazine subscribers and try to improve the response rate by mailing only to those in specific zip codes that in the past had been shown to respond well. Thus, a list that might have been unprofitable to mail to can now produce a positive return. (List enhancement gets a lot more sophisticated than that.)

But, I wonder if Harry and David ever tested how their gift catalog performed when mailed to people named Harry, Harriet, David, Davey, and other variations? The research would predict a better response for those names than names like Sam, Zeke, or Susan. Similarly, Frontgate might see a small improvement when mailing to people named Frank Smith or Susan Fremont.

Enhanced Personalization

We know that personalization works, but what if a marketing pitch personalized some other elements. For example, a database of customer testimonials could be developed, and a testimonial that matched the initial or name of the prospect could be selected. Would I respond better to a marketing piece that featured a satisfied customer named Roger Jones versus one that used Miranda Smith? I'd like to think not, but the research shows I probably would.

Similarly, a featured product might be chosen based on the name of the prospect. A gift catalog might put a Cuisinart product on pitches to prospects whose names started with C and a KitchenAid item to those whose names began with K.

Birthday Fun

If people are attracted by their own birthday numbers, what if one incorporated a seemingly random but prominent number on a mailing? Perhaps a house address on an illustration? If you knew the prospect's birthday was December 14, the number could be 1214. Building this in subtly but visibly would be a challenge, but it could be done.

These are, of course, weak effects. In many cases, employing an implicit egotism strategy would likely not be effective enough to justify its cost. Still, marketers could test the concept, or even research it using past sales data. Direct marketers, in particular, are great at data analysis, and it wouldn't be difficult for a sophisticated marketer to see if people named Harry outperformed those with other names in their last big mailing.

78

Expect More, and Get It!

BRAIN STUDIES ARE providing new insights into consumer behavior, but one of the most important findings is the potential impact of marketing on the actual customer experience. Few advertising and marketing executives discount the value of marketing, but how often have you heard these kinds of statements?

Our product will sell itself!

Once people try the product, they'll love it!

We count on advertising mainly to build awareness.

Many business executives assume that marketing is a front-end activity designed to entice people to buy the product at least once. At that point, the product itself takes over; the customer will like it, or not, and future purchases will depend on which it is. That's true, as far as it goes, but it neglects an important fact: *the customer's real experience with the product will be shaped by his or her expectations and beliefs about the product.*

Note that I'm not saying that the customer's reported experience is affected by preconceived notions; for example, it's common for consumers to rationalize an expensive purchase and report higher levels of satisfaction than are really accurate. I'm saying that the customer's actual experience—before any rationalization or even conscious thought occurs—is affected by what that person knows about the product!

The basis for this bold assertion is research on wine, of all things. Wine is actually a good product to study, because most people aren't wine experts and hence are more suggestible. Following are a few data points that illustrate what I'm talking about.

Price Influences Taste

In Chapter 6, we discussed research that showed people's brains lit up more in the part of the brain that registers a pleasant experience when they thought they were drinking a $45 wine instead of a $5 wine, even though the two wines were actually the same! The subjects anticipated a better experience from the $45 wine, and they got it. Expensive wine really does taste better, even when it isn't![12]

Wine Label Makes Food Better

Another study found that diners offered a free glass of wine from "Noah's Winery in California" ate more food at a fixed-price French restaurant and were even more likely to book a new reservation than diners who were given a glass from "Noah's Winery in North Dakota." As in the previously described experiment, the wine was actually the same for all diners.[13]

Expectation Becomes Reality

What this research shows is that what customers believe about a product can turn into reality—if they believe a product is better, it *will* be better. If you want to look at it another way, if customers have doubts about a product, as in the case of North Dakotan wine, the experience can be diminished. (This would certainly be a frustrating situation for a real North Dakota winery, whose customers would find that their wine never tasted quite as good as that from California or France—even if objectively the wines were equivalent!)

A New Role for Marketing

Critics often assume that marketing, advertising, and branding efforts are intended to manipulate consumers into buying things they don't need. A more common (and benign) view is that these activities are geared to informing consumers about products that they may enjoy or that may improve their lives in some way. Individual marketers could add to this list with specifics such as encouraging repeat purchases, building brand awareness, and so on.

Here's the role that won't be on any of those lists: *establishing high customer expectations that will improve their actual experience with the product or service*. But it should be. The wine research shows that what consumers believe—"Expensive wines are likely to taste better than cheap ones" or "California wines are famous worldwide, and I didn't even know that wines from North Dakota existed"—affects their satisfaction with the product beyond the actual characteristics of the product itself.

It's not a big leap to assert that what a customer knows about a brand will similarly affect the product experience. Lexus traditionally ranks near the top of customer satisfaction surveys. Certainly, the actual quality of the vehicles plays a role in this. But there are a host of other factors—the reputation of the brand, the premium price, the unusually well-appointed dealerships—that create the expectation of a superior-quality product. As long as the product itself doesn't disappoint in some major way, the Lexus buyer is likely to really be more satisfied than had he or she purchased a comparable Toyota.

Product Still Counts

It would be nice to think that good marketing could create a fantastic customer experience on its own, but that's obviously not the case. If a customer buys a $100 wine and it tastes like vinegar, the expectation of an outstanding wine experience will be crushed by the reality of the awful flavor.

A small amount of dissonance between expectation and reality can be overcome, but if the gap is too wide, all bets are off. The customer will realize that the expectation was wrong, and indeed, may find the product worse than it really is. Buying a $5 bottle of wine that has an unpleasant flavor is an experience likely to be forgotten in a day, but buying a $50 bottle from a famous winery that tastes like spoiled cork is likely to create both an immediate high level of dissatisfaction and a long-term suspicion of that brand.

In my opinion, the product must fall in the general range of expectations for marketing to improve customers' real experience. In addition, the expertise of customers will determine how much they will be affected by preconceived notions. The more knowledge and experience customers have, the more they will use objective factors in judging a product. A professional wine taster is unlikely to be fooled by putting a French label and a $100 price tag on last Tuesday's bottling of Two Buck Chuck.

But even pros can be influenced, of course—think of the audiophiles who reported better sound from bizarre accessories like "balancing stones," little rocks reputed to improve sound quality if strategically placed on audio components. It's all a matter of degree; the professional wine taster might easily reject $3 plonk but might be convinced that a good wine was a bit better than it really is with the right priming.

From Wine to Software

Microsoft's much reviled operating system, Vista, suffered from bad press from the time it was introduced. Early users encountered bugs, corporate information technology (IT) executives noisily demanded that they be allowed to keep using Vista's predecessor, Windows XP, and Apple heaped scorn on Vista with its I'm a PC; I'm a Mac ads.

Even after initial bugs were cured, opinions about Vista were still negative compared with past introductions of new Windows versions. This was no doubt annoying to Microsoft executives, just as if a North Dakota winery was shipping superb wine but people still found it less tasty than inferior wine from California. So, in a move out of the neuromarketing playbook, Microsoft conducted a study that asked people to test-drive and rate a new operating system, "Mojave." The new operating system was, of course, actually Vista.

Lo and behold, software users turned out to be as impressionable as wine drinkers and the rest of humanity. An impressive 94 percent of the users rated Mojave higher than they had rated Vista, and Mojave (post-demo) scored 8.5 on a scale of 10 versus Vista, which was scored at 4.4 (pre-demo).[14]

Brainfluence Takeaway: Set High but Achievable Expectations

Be sure your marketing is geared not only to getting customers to buy your product but to improving their experience once they try it. That means setting high but realistic expectations for the product's quality, taste, performance, or whatever measures apply to it. Brand positioning should emphasize those variables that will lead to a positive customer experience; place less emphasis on low prices or value and more on superior flavor, fine craftsmanship, and so on. If you succeed, you'll have happier customers and, of course, higher sales.

79

Surprise Your Customers!

WHAT DOES IT take to make you happy? Not much. A classic study by psychologist Norbert Schwarz found that 10 cents would do the trick. He and his cohorts repeatedly placed a dime near a copy machine where they knew it would be found. When the subjects who found the dime were surveyed shortly after their discovery, their overall satisfaction with life was substantially higher than other subjects who did not find a coin.

Although the original study was conducted back in 1987, when a dime bought more than it does today, the basic idea remains the same: even a tiny positive surprise can improve one's outlook, albeit temporarily. In an interview with the *Baltimore Sun*, Schwarz noted, "It's not the value of what you find. It's that something positive happened to you."[15]

Another study showed that food surprises worked too. In a grocery store, shoppers were asked about their satisfaction with their home TV. Those who had received a free food sample minutes earlier were happier with their TV than those who didn't get the sample.

Brainfluence Takeaway: Create Positive Feelings With a Small Surprise

This study shows that one has the opportunity to create an association of improved mood with a brand if a small positive surprise can be delivered at the same time as a brand impression. And it doesn't have to be a total surprise—receiving a food sample at a grocery store isn't exactly a shocking occurrence.

Here are a few that come to mind.

Sampling, but With Clear Brand Identity

Sampling is pervasive these days in supermarkets and warehouse stores, but often the brand identity is lost in the shuffle. Sampling in a venue not already flooded with sampling stations, ensuring that the display shows the brand, and training the attendant to mention the brand by name will further help ensure the brand gets the boost.

Surprise in the Box

Product makers could include a small, inexpensive free accessory or promotional item in the product package. Obviously, putting "Free gift inside!" on the outside of the box will kill any surprise. But, calling the item a "free gift" *inside* the box would emphasize that it is of some value or utility and likely enhance the surprise.

Shipping Upgrades

Zappos.com became a billion-dollar company in part by surprising its customers with free shipping upgrades. When most of its shoe-selling competitors were taking three or more days to deliver product, Zappos delivered many of its orders using two-day or overnight shipping. Rather than touting a free upgrade policy, they surprised their customers by notifying them of an upgrade after the order had been placed.

Eleven

Gender Brainfluence

RESEARCH CONTINUES TO show that not only do men and women behave differently, but they even use their brains differently. For example, brain scan studies show that men and women viewing an emotional movie show different patterns of brain activation at the same points in the film.[1]

Needless to say, these differences can have major implications for marketers. This section will look at some specific ways to appeal to each gender.

80

Mating on the Mind

A PROFESSOR AT the University of New Mexico has an interesting suggestion: the evolution of the human brain was largely driven by finding better ways to appeal to the opposite sex.

Geoffrey Miller, an evolutionary psychologist, thinks that the human brain is a lot like the peacock's tail—it's a biological artifact that evolved to attract a mate. The brain, of course, has a lot more functionality than a decorative plume of feathers. Sill, Miller thinks the advanced features of the human brain, like language and complex reasoning, are all about sex.

Miller studied conspicuous consumption and altruism. These concepts seem like opposites; the first behavior is selfish, and the second seems generous. Miller thinks they are related, though, and that visible altruism is a form of conspicuous consumption.

To test this idea, Miller and fellow researchers primed two groups of subjects in different ways. The first group was romantically primed by having to write about their ideal date. The second group's assigned topic was the weather.

Each subject was then given an imaginary budget of both money ($5,000) and time (60 hours) to spend. The romantically primed men turned into wild spenders, while the women in that group volunteered like crazy. The men did little volunteering, and the women spent little money.

The neutrally primed group showed no major tendency toward spending or volunteering. The researchers concluded that men and women do "show off" when romantically primed but use different strategies. Guys buy stuff, and women help others.[2]

A follow-up study looked at the degree to which this showing off was visible and found that romantically primed men focused on buying things they could wear or drive and tended to ignore items that would stay in their home. The women in that state chose volunteer activities that were in public settings and avoided solitary tasks.

Those subjects who weren't romantically primed were mostly indifferent to the public or private nature of their spending and volunteering.

Brainfluence Takeaway: Use Romantic Priming if Your Product (or Service Project) Is Conspicuous

Succeed With Men

Long before neuromarketing and evolutionary psychology, marketers knew that men spend money to enhance their reputation (and their appeal to the opposite sex)—expensive sports cars, costly restaurants, and so on, all demonstrate that the guy is financially well fixed and, because of that, attractive.

Marketers who give a man a chance to buy something expensive in a visible way can expect an above-average rate of success. Nonprofits looking for donations must, to appeal to males, also ensure visibility; public recognition is particularly important among those who (usually unconsciously) are seeking to boost their attractiveness.

Succeed With Women

The female side of the equation is a bit different. Women, apparently, tend not to spend money conspicuously as an implicit mating strategy. (They may still spend money on clothing and accessories intended to enhance their attractiveness, but romantic priming doesn't have much effect.)

Interestingly, they may be induced to spend their *time* conspicuously for that purpose. Nonprofits looking for volunteers know that recognition is important, and this research underscores that some recognition should be public and visible to be most effective.

How does one accomplish romantic priming outside a psychology lab? Probably the most logical way is with gender-appropriate images that put the viewer in a mating frame of mind. We'll see in subsequent chapters some specific ways this effect has been demonstrated.

81

Guys Like It Simple

POPULAR BOOKS LIKE *Men Are from Mars, Women Are from Venus*, not to mention generations of comedians, have played up the differences between males and females. What's not a joke is that researchers at Northwestern University and the University of Haifa found that there are provable biological differences in the way that boys and girls process language in their brains.[3,4]

The researchers found that language processing by girls is more abstract, whereas boys are more sensory when dealing with that task. Boys and girls use different parts of the brains for the same activities.

The researchers focused on the educational implications of their research. The differences in language processing were dramatic enough that they suggested that single-gender classes might be more effective. They also suggested that boys might perform better on written exams about material they had read and on oral exams for material they had absorbed by hearing it.

The findings suggest that boys may have some kind of sensory processing bottleneck that prevents auditory or visual information from reaching the language areas of the brain.

The researchers extend this as a possible explanation for use of more complex and abstract communications by women. They use giving directions as one example; women, they say, tend to provide more detail, like describing what kind of landmarks are near a turn, while men use less detail.

J. Peterman Is From Mars, the Catalog Copy Isn't

This theory would suggest that advertising copy aimed at males should be simple and direct and that female-oriented copy can provide more context. The first brand that popped into my head while pondering simple copy versus highly contextual and abstract copy was J. Peterman, whose catalog features highly engaging but hardly simple and direct copy. I tracked down the percentage of female versus male customers for the J. Peterman catalog (which includes items for both men and women and whose flagship product is a men's duster coat), and I wasn't surprised that females outnumbered males by more than a two-to-one margin.

Obviously, the product selection has something to do with this skewed gender split in J. Peterman's customer base, but another explanation is that the lengthy product narratives work better with the firm's primary gender demographic: females. Indeed, catalog marketing is highly scientific: the detailed statistics for both products and customer demographics ensure a Darwinian evolution over the years.

A big caution, though: the gender differences in language processing among 9- to 15-year-olds are well demonstrated by this research; adult differences and their real-world implications are a lot more speculative at this point. And overall statistical differences don't say much about individuals—I enjoy reading the J. Peterman descriptions as much as the next guy . . . or gal!

Brainfluence Takeaway: Use Simple Copy for Guys

Wordy copy is rarely a good idea, but especially if you are aiming at a male audience, in which case, keep the prose simple. Typically, guys process language in a less abstract, more sensory way, and excess verbiage will get in the way of your message.

82

Are Women Better at Sales?

HAVE YOU NOTICED that female salespeople seem to dominate some areas and that these women seem to skew toward the attractive end of the spectrum? One example is the pharmaceutical sales rep, who prototypically is an attractive woman who spends much of her time calling on a predominantly male physician customer base. That's an overgeneralization, of course; there are many female doctors and plenty of male drug reps. Still, the stereotype is sufficiently valid that a physician acquaintance of mine expressed mock shock at seeing a middle-aged male drug rep, quipping, "I don't think I've seen one of those before."

Here are a few theories I've heard advanced as to why female salespeople might be more successful:

■ *Getting in the door?* Some might think that the reason for the dominance of female reps in some areas is their "get in the door" factor.

Here's how that theory might work: if a busy male executive has a new salesperson waiting in the lobby, is he more likely to make the time to see a paunchy middle-aged guy or an attractive 20-something woman? That might seem like a no-brainer to some, but we don't have any actual data on that.

- *People skills?* Another reason for the success of female salespeople might be better people skills. In fact, there's an entire book devoted to that theory: *Women Make the Best Salesmen: Isn't It Time You Started Using Their Secrets?* The book's description notes, "Women, with their natural social skills and acute emotional antennae, have natural advantages both sexes can learn from."[5]

Another Theory—The Peacock Display

Could the mere presence of a halfway attractive female serve to romantically prime the male customer? Based on the research we previously wrote about, if subconsciously primed with romantic thoughts, the male customer will be more inclined to demonstrate his mating potential by his spending behavior, for example, by placing a large order.

We know that stimuli as trivial as a photo of an attractive woman have a romantic priming effect on men (see page 90). It's no leap at all to suggest that a real woman would work at least as well. And, if you buy into Geoffrey Miller's theory, you would expect that other behavior, such as placing an order, would serve the same peacock display purpose.

In the medical sphere, even though a physician usually isn't actually ordering product or spending money (patients and insurance companies spend the real money), he can still demonstrate his power and mastery by agreeing to distribute samples, recommend the product in appropriate situations, and so on. Exercising authority in this manner seems as much of a visible display as writing a check.

I'm not suggesting anything improper is occurring. Although it's possible that either party could engage in overtly flirtatious behavior, I don't think that occurs in most situations or is even necessary for the romantic priming effect to work. Indeed, such behavior could be counterproductive.

Of course, *many* factors influence the typical decision-making process, most of them substantive. The product has to be appropriate and more or less as good as the competition. The price has to be in line with expectations and the competition. Sales skills—the ability to present the product effectively and establish a bond with the customer—are important as well. Sending in an attractive salesperson with an inadequate product or poor training is likely to fail most of the time.

I view the romantic priming effect as a tiebreaker; given two firms with similar products and pricing, the salesperson who can create the romantic priming effect may have a small advantage when asking for the order. Think of it as a temporary and subtle reality distortion field. Any influence on judgment will most likely occur in the presence of the salesperson when the priming effect is maximized. When the salesperson moves to close the deal, if the customer was favorably disposed to begin with, the subtle and unconscious priming influence might, for example, be enough to produce an immediate signature instead of a promise to think about it.

A Male Approach

Female salespeople aren't the only ones who try to appeal to male customers for a "power display." I've periodically received calls from boiler-room security salesmen (universally male, in my experience) trying to pitch a stock or at least get an agreement that I'll listen to future pitches. I'm usually courteous when I disengage a telemarketer, but the only way to get these guys off the line is to hang up. Any attempt to end the call will produce more rapid-fire questions.

One approach I've had them use is a line such as, "Are you telling me you can't make a $5,000 investment?" Said dismissively, it's clearly intended to question the authority, the financial wherewithal, and ultimately the masculinity of the client. The desired response is another peacock display, perhaps something like, "Of course I can! I make much larger investments all the time!" With that response, the sales guy is back on track with his pitch. Not romantic priming, perhaps, but another way to produce a similar result. In avian terms, he's asking, "Do you actually have any tail feathers at all?"

The Good News

With entire books devoted to explaining why women make better salespeople, one might fear discrimination in the hiring, retention, and promotion process. In the sales profession, though, it's results that count. Few companies retain ineffective salespeople, and many base a significant portion of the individual's compensation on actual sales metrics. Theoretically, at least, that should make gender discrimination much less likely than in more subjectively evaluated positions. Ultimately, too, customers want salespeople who can fix their problems and make their lives easier—appearance and gender factors will pale in comparison to real solutions.

Brainfluence Takeaway: Exploit the Peacock Effect With Male Buyers

Romantic priming can affect the sales process, although it may be a second-order effect in most situations. A salesperson seeking to exploit that small advantage should make a subtle appeal to the (male) customer's financial or authority status. In most cases, it shouldn't be as aggressive as, "Are you telling me you can't afford the payments on this car?"

Rather, a lower-key approach such as, "Would the payments on this car be comfortable for you?" will give the customer a chance to show off his beautiful tail feathers. A simple question like, "Can you sign off on this yourself?" can provide the same kind of opportunity (if he *can* sign off on it himself). Linking the display of financial ability or decision-making power to a concrete action, such as signing an agreement, is the final element in turning any possible priming effect into sales success.

83

Do Women Make Men Crazy?

DO WOMEN MAKE men crazy? It turns out pictures of women *do* have an effect on male decision making. The guys don't actually become crazy, but they become more impatient and focused on the short term.

Evolutionary psychologists Margo Wilson and Martin Daly (both of McMaster University) studied this phenomenon and concluded that pictures of attractive women were causing men to value short-term benefits more by putting them in a mating frame of mind. A clever experimental plan demonstrated the priming effect of photos of attractive women.[6]

The researchers evaluated the degree to which subjects discounted the future. We all discount the value of future benefits versus immediate or short-term benefits—it's logical. Most of us would choose to have $100 given to us immediately versus, say, $105 in two years. Every individual has his or her own discount rate for making these kinds of decisions. Men, as a group, have a higher discount rate than women; that is, their preferences skew toward shorter-term rewards.

Wilson and Daly think evolutionary psychology accounts for this difference, as a basic tenet of that field is that women operate with a longer time frame due to the realities of childbearing and subsequent care.

Wilson and Daly tested this hypothesis by showing men and women head shots of attractive and unattractive members of the opposite sex. Men who viewed photos of women judged to be attractive showed a significant increase in their discount rate; that is, they became more attracted by short-term rewards. The other groups did not show statistically significant changes. (See related findings about bikini photos on page 90.)

Other recent research even showed a link between mating priming and warlike instincts in young men. Photos of attractive women served to prime men to respond more quickly to images or words related to war. As seems common in these experiments, women were unaffected by such images.[7]

Brainfluence Takeaway: Attractive Female Photos Shorten Male Time Horizons

Male viewers are influenced by photos of attractive women, and their decisions skew toward the short-term and impulsive. Incorporating such images in marketing or point-of-sale materials has the potential to lift sales if the product itself has an appropriate reward.

I would expect that sales of apparel or grooming products would do better than, say, broccoli. The work done by Wilson and Daly specifically looked at monetary rewards, which would have most significance for products such as loans, insurance, investments, casinos, and so forth.

When Not to Use Pretty Women

I'd also expect that photos of attractive women would be ineffective or even a negative when selling certain kinds of products to men. For example, products like life insurance and annuities both involve spending current money for a future (and, in the case of insurance, uncertain) payout. Priming male sales prospects with mating cues could be counterproductive by making the cash in their pocket seem more valuable than future rewards.

SECTION

Twelve

Shopper Brainfluence

84

Cooties in Every Bag

SOME OF US are old enough to remember when supermarkets sold food and a few household products, drugstores sold health and beauty products, hardware stores sold hardware, and so on. Today, any number of chains have huge stores that stock just about every category imaginable.

I recall the first megastore I shopped at: it was fascinating to watch what other shoppers had in their carts as they checked out—a gallon of milk, a floor mop, khaki slacks, and a chain saw . . . great fodder for a creative writing contest! It turns out that there's a downside to some of those weird product juxtapositions. Research shows that products that trigger subconscious feelings of disgust can contaminate consumer perceptions of other products.

Products such as lard, feminine hygiene items, cigarettes, and cat litter trigger a disgust reaction, as do some less obvious items, such as mayonnaise and shortening. The research, conducted by Gavan Fitzsimons, a professor of marketing and psychology at Duke University, and Andrea Morales, an assistant professor of marketing at Arizona State, examined how products like these affected consumer perceptions of other items in their shopping carts.[1]

The experiment was simple. The researchers placed food products next to a product that would trigger a disgust reaction and let subjects see the products. They then tested the subjects' attitudes and found that food items that had been in proximity to a disgust-inducing item were less appealing. (Apparently, cooties can't jump very far. If the products were one inch or more apart, the effect was negligible.)

This wasn't a fleeting effect, either. Even an hour later, fewer people wanted to try a cookie if they had seen it in contact with a package of feminine hygiene products. The researchers attribute this behavior to a human instinct to avoid consuming items that might be contaminated.

Fat Transfer

One of the stranger findings was that rice cakes in a transparent package were judged to have a higher fat content after subjects saw them touching a container of lard. The fat gain experienced by the rice cakes was lower when they were in an opaque package. It appears that products in clear packaging are the most vulnerable to subconscious contamination.

Brainfluence Takeaway: Watch Your Pairings

Clearly, marketers can't control what shoppers combine in their shopping carts, and once the item is in the cart, the consumer is almost certain to buy it anyway. It's also doubtful that this negative association is a long-lasting effect that would tarnish the brand or the consumer's long-term feelings about the product.

I'd worry more about preshopping cart product contagion on the store shelves and in displays. Fortunately, most stores segregate their products by category, and one won't find cat litter in the cookie aisle. But, particularly in smaller environments, weird juxtapositions can occur. In a hotel "convenience store," I spied cups of "Instant Lunch" noodles directly touching packages of feminine hygiene products. Just a guess, but I'd expect those noodles to be slow sellers.

Clear (and Present) Danger

Marketers should be mindful of this previously unknown downside to clear packaging. Although complete transparency ensures consumers that the product they are buying is exactly what they expect, it seems that clear packaging causes greater vulnerability to imaginary contamination.

In retail environments that aren't well lit and spotlessly clean, it seems likely that clear packages might allow the products to be "infected" (subconsciously, of course) by their surroundings. So, for products likely to be sold in widely varied environments with uncertain maintenance (convenience stores, gas stations, etc.), opt for opaque packages to keep the product free from imagined contamination.

85

Customer Replies Change Minds

It's axiomatic that you find out how good a business really is when it has already screwed up once; the speed and nature of the fix show the firm's true nature. After shipping you the wrong item, do they just offer to refund your return shipping? Do they overnight the correct item to you, no questions asked? How quickly do they resolve the problem?

It turns out that the way companies respond to bad online reviews makes a difference too. A Harris survey showed that 18 percent of those who posted a negative review of the merchant and received a reply ultimately became loyal customers and bought more.[2]

In addition, nearly 70 percent of those consumers receiving replies reversed the negative content either by deleting the bad review or posting a second positive one. Considering the power of word of mouth—in particular, negative word of mouth—that's a stunning accomplishment.

Although salvaging one out of five unhappy customers is a laudable goal (and, I suspect, a lot cheaper than prospecting for new customers), I have no doubt the benefits extend far beyond that number. Countless other buyers reading reviews will see a proactive response to a problem instead of an unanswered (and apparently ignored) complaint. (Indeed, when I'm evaluating an online purchase I usually visit the firm's forum to see how quickly and effectively they respond to problem reports. Unanswered complaints are a huge red flag.)

Brainfluence Takeaway: Engage Problem Customers Quickly

Monitor where your customers post—Twitter, Facebook, blogs, review sites, your own support forum, and so on—and engage them quickly and constructively. Don't try to win an argument about who's right; if the customer is upset, that will just create aggravation and ill will. Offer a simple but sincere apology, and state how the problem can be resolved with minimal customer pain. Not only do you have a chance to retain that customer, but you'll have influenced many others as well. Even better, with a great response you may influence the customer to remove or correct the initial complaint.

86

It's Wise to Apologize

OCCASIONALLY, PRODUCT OR service failures go viral. The "United Breaks Guitars" video (www.youtube.com/watch?v=5YGc4zOqozo) is one example. After baggage attendants at United Airlines broke a musician's guitar and the customer service staff provided no satisfaction, he recorded a video that has garnered more than 10 million views to date.

A little older example is the "Yours Is a Very Bad Hotel" slide show (www.slideshare.net/whatidiscover/yours-is-a-very-bad-hotel-97480) directed at the Doubletree Club Houston, which recounts the hotel's indifference encountered by a pair of business travelers when their confirmed reservations weren't honored.

Much like the million-dollar pickle story (see page 179), these incidents share a common thread: an initial customer service failure was exacerbated by poor treatment after it happened. The guitar video portrays United Airlines customer service as indifferent and uncaring. The Doubletree slide show mocks "night clerk Mike" in hilarious fashion; Mike had not only given away their rooms, but he took no responsibility for the problem and found them rooms at another hotel only under duress from the weary travelers. In each case, a prompt and friendly resolution of the problem would have ended the incident before it turned into a public relations problem.

The Price of Rude Behavior

In *The Upside of Irrationality*, Dan Ariely describes an experiment that shows how customer attitudes can be changed by a simple apology.

Like many of Ariely's experiments, this one was deceptively simple. Subjects were recruited with a promise of a $5 payment for completing a brief task. To measure their attitude toward the researcher (or research organization), the researcher "accidentally" overpaid each subject by a few dollars at the end of the task in a way that the subject could easily pocket the difference. For half the subjects, the researcher explained the task and paid the subjects after it was complete. With the other subjects, he interrupted the explanation to take an unrelated and unimportant cell phone call and offered no explanation or apology when he resumed the instructions. In both cases he paid the subjects, suggested they count the money, and then moved away.

Although the faux call took a mere 12 seconds, the rude treatment dramatically affected the subjects' willingness to return the overpayment for the task. Whereas 45 percent of the regular group pointed out the error and returned the extra money, just 14 percent of the phone call group did so. A few seconds of rudeness, and the portion of honest customers dropped by two thirds.

Ariely considers rude treatment to be a revenge motivator. "He was rude to me, so I'm justified in paying him back." In this case, payback meant *not* paying back the extra money. An attitude change can manifest itself in many ways in the real world. Customers might complain, they might be rude in return, they might post derogatory reviews or negative social media comments, or they might attempt to take advantage of the company in some other way as compensation for their poor treatment. If the company is particularly unlucky, these disgruntled customers will have the talent and motivation to create something that reaches far beyond their own circle of friends.

The Apology Effect

So what's a company to do? Ariely conducted a second experiment that added a third condition: the researcher took the cell phone call, but immediately apologized for the behavior. The data showed a startling change: the group that received the apology returned the overpayment at the same rate as those in the "no interruption" group. The apology negated the effect of the rude behavior immediately preceding it.

Brainfluence Takeaway: Don't Be Afraid to Apologize

Ariely's simple experiment confirms what customer service experts know already: a sincere apology goes a long way toward defusing customer anger. Sometimes companies and their staffers are reluctant to apologize, as doing so is an admission of fault. That's a mistake. Customers are more likely to continue to fight, whether that means filing a lawsuit or creating a viral complaint video, if they meet with unapologetic indifference.

87

The Power of Touch

HAVE YOU EVER been in a store and had a salesperson encourage you to hold an item and perhaps even imagine what it would be like to own it? In 2003, the Illinois Attorney General actually warned consumers to be wary of this practice. Although that might sound like the ultimate in nanny-state government, subsequent research showed that touching an item did indeed cause people to feel a greater sense of ownership and to place a higher value on it. Imagining that they owned it increased the effect.

Marketing professors Joann Peck and Suzanne Shu evaluated how subjects felt about items with and without touching them and also with and without visualizing they owned them. In a series of experiments involving products such as a Slinky and a mug, they found touching did change attitudes.[3]

Psychological Ownership

Ownership can take different forms. You may feel a sense of ownership in the company you work for, your alma mater, or favorite sports team, even though you have no legal ownership in any of them. Physical objects can be the same; you know they aren't yours, but you can have varying levels of feeling ownership for them. Separate from a sense of owning an item, you can also feel positive or negative emotion toward it.

Peck and Shu found that touching an object immediately improved both the level of perceived ownership and positive emotion. The only exception was an object that had an unpleasant surface. People still felt more ownership, but they didn't like the item any more.

Brainfluence Takeaway: Let Customers Touch Your Product

You have a greater chance of making a sale if you let your customers touch or hold your product (unless it is unpleasant to touch, a condition that you might want to address anyway). You can amplify the effect by helping customers imagine that they own the product.

Small toys and mugs were the experimental props, but the findings could extend to larger and more expensive items. Getting customers behind the wheel will certainly provide tactile stimuli. Asking a few questions such as, "Can you imagine pulling into your driveway and garage in this car?" would provide the ownership imagery to amplify the effect.

Brand flagship stores, ranging from Apple to Gucci, all serve the important purpose of getting potential customers to handle the products in a controlled and positive setting. Get your product into your customers' hands, and it's more likely they'll leave with it.

88

When Difficulty Sells

MARKETERS EXPEND A great deal of effort making it easy to buy their products. They expand distribution channels, offer financing alternatives, and when possible, ensure the customer can leave with the product at time of purchase. After all, if you think of the sales process as a funnel (or perhaps a leaky funnel), every little barrier to purchasing is one more way to knock that potential buyer out of the funnel. The exceptions to this rule are some true luxury products.

Want to buy a Ferrari? Write a check and get on the waiting list. Any number of high-end luxury products are sold only through a small number of brand-controlled retail stores, which means that the potential buyer must travel to that city and a specific location to make a purchase. Other luxury items have different ways of making buying their product an ordeal.

Instead of going out of business, though, most of the difficult-to-buy brands are highly prized by their owners. One reason for this is cognitive dissonance. In this context, it means that our brains have to make sense of this conflict:

1. Obtaining this product was inconvenient.
2. I'm smart, and wouldn't expend a lot of effort to buy just any product.

The resolution that our brain usually comes up with is:

This is an amazing product, and it's more than worth the effort it took to buy it.

Some of the early research in cognitive dissonance resolution took place more than 50 years ago. Stanford University researchers conducted an experiment in which subjects who wanted to join a discussion group went through an initiation process in which they had to read to the group. Some subjects were in a "severe" group that read sexually explicit (hence embarrassing) text, while a "mild" group read neutral text. All of the subjects then heard a recording of other group members in which the conversation was intentionally as dull as possible. The researchers found that the subjects who underwent the severe initiation rated the discussion as significantly more interesting than those in the mild group.[4]

The cognitive dissonance factor doesn't just affect ultra-luxury products. It's one reason why, for example, Apple fanatics stood in line for hours to buy the latest iteration of the iPhone, even though it required the often-reviled AT&T phone service. Obviously, the product itself is great, but the fanaticism of true Apple diehards and their unwillingness to tolerate any criticism of the product is clearly a result of their cognitive dissonance resolution. And there's likely a feedback loop effect: the true believers who line up the night before a product launch are already disposed to like the product, and the extreme effort they put into purchasing the product reinforces that affinity.

Not all luxury brands pursue this strategy. Lexus, for example, strives to make the buying experience as painless as possible. (Of course, some would consider Lexus to be a premium brand, not a luxury brand.)

Brainfluence Takeaway: Easy Isn't *Always* Best

For most brands and situations, eliminating obstacles to buying is a good thing. But the counterintuitive strategy from cognitive dissonance research suggests that easy isn't *always* best. If you are lucky enough to have a highly sought-after product, you may actually *increase* buyer commitment to your product by making the buying process a little more difficult.

Conversely, if you find yourself in a situation in which your customers find that buying is difficult, for example, if there's an unexpected shortage of a popular product, try to turn the problem into a plus: use it as an indicator of the popularity of the product. The combination of cognitive dissonance and social proof will make for highly committed customers.

Thirteen

Video, TV, and Film Brainfluence

89

Don't Put the CEO on TV

WHY DO SPOKESPEOPLE in ads who aren't professional actors do so badly most of the time? No doubt we've all seen the painfully bad ads featuring the sales manager of the local car dealer or the guy who owns the furniture outlet.

Of course, there are a few success stories: long-running campaigns that turned chief executive officers (CEOs) into celebrities and changed the fortunes of the company—Lee Iacocca's series of Chrysler ads comes to mind, along with Dave Thomas's Wendy's commercials. Part of the reason is the level of production involved; filming national spots for an auto company will have a high-quality director who will use as many takes as required to get it right. Local retail ads have lower production values and will probably use the first take in which the "actor" doesn't muff the lines.

Neuroscience suggests another reason for this divide.

In filming a commercial featuring a spokesperson, the primary focus is usually on the text the actor will deliver—why the new product is great, how prices have been slashed for the huge weekend sale, and so on. Research shows, however, that gestures and body language may be as important as the words and that a mismatch between the verbal and physical means of communication causes a shift in brain waves similar to the reaction to misused or unexpected words.

Neuroscientist Spencer D. Kelly of Colgate University studies the effects of gestures by measuring event-related potentials—brain waves that form peaks and valleys. Measured with an EEG, the patterns show how different areas of the brain process information. One particular valley, or negative peak, has been dubbed N400; it occurs when we stumble over an inappropriate word. (For example, "He spread his toast with socks.")[1]

Interestingly, the same N400 negative peak is found when a speaker's gestures don't match the words being spoken. For example, if the speaker was saying "tall" but using gestures that indicated something short, a strong negative peak would be observed. The researchers interpreted this as meaning that speech and gestures are processed simultaneously and that observers factor the meaning of the gesture into their interpretation of the word.

Our Bodies Talk

Years ago, the term *body language* was popularized when various authors offered interpretations for different body positions and gestures. Crossed arms meant resistance to an idea, steepled fingers were a symbol of authority, and so on. Readers were encouraged to pay attention to the body language of others and behave in accord with their better understanding of the mental frame of the other person. For example, faced with a sales prospect leaning back from the table with crossed arms, a salesperson would be foolish to plow ahead touting features and benefits; the first step would be to get the subject in a more receptive frame of mind.

The fact is that people are constantly processing the body language and gestures of others, but this is done mostly at the unconscious level. When we say, "That salesperson seemed a bit sketchy," it may well be due to a mismatch between the words being spoken and the body language.

Some business owners may be comfortable enough as actors to do a credible job. In many cases, they have one advantage over a professional actor: they know their product and believe in it. If this essential truth can be communicated to viewers, they don't need exceptional thespian skills. A business owner who can't deliver the lines with complete conviction, though, had better be an outstanding actor. How many times have we heard car dealers claim they are having the "sale of the century," with prices that are "the lowest in our history," and that will "never be seen again." A few weeks later, of course, we hear a different variation on the same theme. Delivering these lines with heartfelt conviction might be best left to a professional.

Brainfluence Takeaway: Physical Actions Outweigh Words

In every element of your marketing campaign—print ads, commercials, and sales presentations—pay as much attention to the physical actions of the people as to what they are saying. If these gestures and postures reinforce the verbal message, that message will be more powerful. If instead the nonverbal cues create dissonance with the intended message, the effectiveness of that effort will drop.

90

Get the Order Right!

ONE OF THE more intriguing concepts in neuromarketing is priming: influencing an individual's behavior by the introduction of various subtle cues. This often occurs in a subliminal manner; that is, the individual is entirely unaware that he or she has received cues of any nature or that his or her behavior has been affected in any way.

In master wordsmith Frank Luntz's *Words That Work*, I ran across a phenomenon that I call priming by order. In a nutshell, research conducted by Luntz and his firm showed that the order in which three films about a political candidate were played dramatically affected perception of that candidate by focus group participants.[2]

Frank Luntz has built a career and a business around advising politicians and corporations how to choose the right words. Although Luntz may come across as a sort of verbal Svengali, most of his recommendations are based on specific research. He doesn't just come up with magic words, like renaming the inheritance tax the death tax or calling drilling for oil energy exploration; he uses polls and focus groups to discover what really works. I've always been a fan of quantitative marketing, so when someone backs up the claims with hard numbers, I tend to listen.

The kind of priming I talk about elsewhere in this book is extremely subtle: individuals are exposed, say, to words or pictures with no particular attention drawn to them. Often, the loaded words or images seem to be part of the general background or are mixed in with neutral content. Subsequently, the behavior of these subjects is observed to be different— a money image on a computer screen saver, for example, causes the individuals who saw it to behave in a more selfish fashion after exposure to it. Luntz describes a somewhat different phenomenon that I think resembles other priming examples.

Luntz's test began as an accident. In 1992, he was showing focus groups three short films of presidential candidate Ross Perot: a biography, testimonials praising Ross Perot, and a recorded speech by Perot himself. In one session, he inadvertently showed the speech first and was stunned to find that the individuals in that group were far more negative about Perot than all of his previous groups.

Further testing showed that leading with the speech was far less effective at creating a positive impression of the candidate. He attributed this to the fact that Perot had an impressive business background and was well respected, but he didn't necessarily communicate this through his personal presence and words. His ideas were a bit different from those of typical politicians too. As Luntz aptly puts it, "Unless and until you knew something about the man and his background, you would get the impression that his mental tray was not quite in the full, upright, and locked position." Luntz lists getting the order right as a key technique for preventing message mistakes.

In one sense, we shouldn't be surprised—sales and marketing are a process, and we wouldn't expect a salesperson to attempt to close the deal before assessing the customer's needs, describing the product benefits, and answering objections. In another sense, though, Luntz's experience *is* a bit startling. In this case, the subjects were passively viewing information of three different types; they all saw all of the content, and there was no interaction to close the deal. Nevertheless, the order of viewing made a huge difference in their opinions even after they had viewed all of the content.

This is clearly an effect that marketers should be aware of; in the Perot case, his credibility was irreparably damaged when viewers were exposed to his somewhat outlandish ideas and grating voice before his credibility had been established by third-party narration and testimonials. Once the viewers were turned off, exposure to the rest of the Perot information didn't turn them back on to him.

Brainfluence Takeaway: Credibility Before Claims

It's common in marketing to lead with a powerful claim to grab the viewer's attention—"The most effective investment management system ever devised!"—and then follow with supporting information. If you buy into the idea of priming by order, it might be more effective to lead with, "Developed by a company that has been managing its clients' money for more than 150 years . . ." or "Described by former Federal Reserve Chairman Alan Greenspan as 'an amazing breakthrough that even I can be exuberant about . . .'" and *then* segue into the actual claims.

Certainly, every situation is different. Perhaps if Perot hadn't been a big-eared short guy without much hair and didn't have a manner of speaking that was part cracker and part nails-on-chalkboard, Luntz's testing of order wouldn't have yielded such dramatic results.

Nevertheless, marketers will ignore these data at their peril; introducing an idea, particularly an idea that might not be instantly believable, and then backing it up may be less effective than preparing the audience to accept it first.

91

Emotion Beats Logic

THE IDEA THAT ads that engage us emotionally work better than those that don't should not be a big shock to anyone who's spent time in advertising. Surprisingly, though, I still encounter business executives who don't believe they are swayed by emotional factors when buying things and often doubt that others are. So, for those uberrational decision makers, here's the hard data.

The UK-based Institute of Practitioners in Advertising (IPA) maintains a data bank of 1,400 case studies of successful advertising campaigns submitted for the IPA Effectiveness Award competition over the past three decades. An analysis of the IPA data compared the profitability boost of campaigns that relied primarily on emotional appeal versus those that used rational persuasion and information. Campaigns with purely emotional content performed about twice as well (31 percent versus 16 percent) with only rational content, and those that were purely emotional did a little better (31 percent versus 26 percent) than those that mixed emotional and rational content.

In their book, *Brand Immortality: How Brands Can Live Long and Prosper*, Hamish Pringle and Peter Field attribute this split to our brain's ability to process emotional input without cognitive processing, as well as our brain's more powerful recording of emotional stimuli.[3]

Pringle and Field note that although an emotional marketing campaign may be more effective, creating ads that engage consumer emotions isn't easy. By comparison, basing a campaign on a "killer fact" (if a brand has such an advantage) is comparatively simple. Indeed, brands have damaged themselves when an emotional campaign failed to align with reality. Pringle and Field suggest that committing to an emotional branding approach be "hardwired into the fabric of the brand," which requires a major commitment as well as good understanding of consumer motivation. They cite Nike's pervasive theme of "success in sport" as an example of a brand that focuses on a key emotional driver and builds advertising, sponsorships, and so on, around it.

Smaller brands may not be able to follow the same emotional branding approach as the market leaders, Pringle and Field note, but they may be able to segment the market to find a group of consumers that will respond to a different appeal. Ben & Jerry's and Jones Soda, for example, weren't the biggest players in their markets, but both achieved success by appealing to smaller segments of consumers.

Smaller entities face additional challenges. Their name recognition is likely much lower, and an emotion-based campaign may befuddle consumers who don't even link the brand and its product category. Budweiser can run amusing and engaging commercials about Clydesdales and Dalmatians because everyone in the audience knows their products, and most know their brand imagery. A small business might have to take the combined rational and emotional approach even if it is slightly less effective, or at least ensure that its emotion-based ads clearly identify the product.

Brainfluence Takeaway: Get Emotional

Emotion-based ads may be more difficult to create, but the statistics say it's worth the effort. Although pure emotional appeals have been shown to work best, using a dual approach that includes some facts may be best for brands that aren't well known to consumers.

SECTION

Fourteen

Brainfluence on the Web

92

First Impressions Count—Really!

THE MAXIM THAT says "First impressions can be deceiving" may apply to websites, but your visitors may not give you a chance to undo a negative first impression.

How long do you think it takes someone to decide whether your website is appealing? A few seconds? Up to a minute? Researchers at Carleton University were stunned to find that showing users an image of a website for a mere 50 milliseconds—that's just a twentieth of a second—was sufficient for them to decide how appealing a website was.[1]

Lest you dismiss this as interesting but not really meaningful for real-world website usage, there were additional findings that hammered home the relevance of that instantaneous impression:

1. The 50-millisecond rating for visual appeal correlated highly with ratings given after much longer exposures.
2. The visual appeal rating was found to correlate highly with other ratings—whether a site was boring or interesting, clear or confusing, and so on.

Confirmation Bias Makes the First Impression Stick

The researchers suggest that there's a confirmation bias at work that amplifies the potency of the first impression. Once our human minds form an opinion, we readily accept new information that agrees with that opinion; we discount or reject contradictory information.

Long-held beliefs related to topics like religion or politics are some of the most powerful examples of confirmation bias. Try carrying on a rational discussion of politics with someone committed to one political party, and that person will likely find a way to discount or dismiss any facts that disagree with his or her beliefs.

In essence, it seems that the opinion of a website's appearance formed in milliseconds biases users as they continue to view the site. If their initial impression was good, flaws they find will be discounted. Conversely, if they disliked the site at first glance, it will be difficult to change that impression by more time on the site.

Happy Users Keep Trying

Human factors expert Don Norman comes to a similar conclusion, albeit from a different perspective. In his book *Emotional Design*, Norman reports on research that shows users who are happy with a design are more apt to find it easier to use. Looking at the underlying neuroscience and psychology, Norman posits that a user in a positive frame of mind (rendered positive by a pleasing and emotionally satisfying design) is more likely to find a way to accomplish the task. A user who is negative or frustrated is more liable to repeat the same action that didn't work the first time. This is a strategy that works only occasionally with physical products and is almost never as successful on websites. Naturally, additional failures cause more frustration and ultimate lack of success.

Brainfluence Takeaway: Test Your Site's First Impression

It would be nice to think that a magic formula exists for making a great first impression. Unfortunately, the study, which used 100 different home pages in their testing, failed to uncover any consistent design characteristics that accounted for high ratings—even though the ratings were fairly consistent across the population of raters.

Naturally, using good designers and empowering them to do their best to create appealing and user-friendly pages is a great start. Testing the design, or alternative designs, on potential site visitors is the only way to really determine visual appeal in the target population.

Beyond the Home Page

Remember, many, if not most, of your site visitors won't arrive on your site's home page. They may come through a landing page because they clicked on a paid ad or a content page that turned up in a search. In addition to testing the home page, spot-check typical entry pages too.

93

Make Your Website Golden

WHAT DO MATHEMATICIANS, architects, sculptors, biologists, and graphic designers have in common? They all use what is perhaps the most interesting number in mathematics: the golden mean, also called the golden ratio and the golden section. Approximated as 1.618 and illustrated as a rectangle in the following graphic, the golden mean plays a prominent role in math, science, and art.

Mathematicians know this number as phi, the ratio between number pairs in the Fibonacci sequence. Biologists find it in the proportions of Nautilus shells and leaves. Architects, painters, and sculptors have

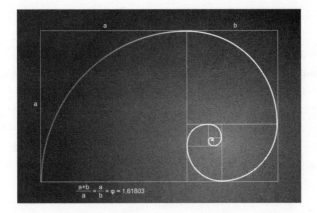

incorporated the ratio into their works because it seems to impart a pleasing balance. The facade of the Parthenon, considered one of the most perfectly proportioned buildings in history, matches the golden ratio. The frequency with which this number seems to pop up in such disparate areas may strike some as surprising, or even a bit spooky.

Neuroscientists are starting to unravel at least a piece of the mystery using functional magnetic resonance imaging (fMRI) brain scans. Italian researchers showed subjects undergoing fMRI brain scans images of sculptures. The original sculptures followed the classical proportions defined by the golden mean. The subjects, who were selected for their lack of detailed art knowledge, also saw images of the same sculptures modified to depart from that ratio. When the subjects viewed the sculptures that followed the golden mean, their brains lit up in a different pattern; one part of the brain where more activity was observed was the insula, an area responsible for mediating emotions. This reaction was judged to be a measure of objective beauty, that is, beauty not influenced by the individual's own taste.[2]

Brainfluence Takeaway: Use the Golden Mean

It's significant that a positive response to specifically proportioned shapes is built into our brains. That doesn't mean that every element on every web page or print ad should have a width-to-height ratio of 1.618.

In some cases, deliberate deviations may have greater impact. After all, ads aren't usually intended to be timeless works of art. Subject matter and available space may impose other dimensional constraints. Nevertheless, graphic designers and commercial artists should be aware of our brains' preference for this proportion and use it when appropriate.

Particularly when we know that visitors make a judgment on a website's visual appeal in a tiny fraction of a second (see page 244), appealing to their brain's innate sense of beauty will help steer that ultrafast decision process.

94

Rich Media Boost Engagement

FOR YEARS, SEARCH engine result pages (SERPs) consisted of 10 blue links, some additional text following each link, and ads that were also usually text links. In the past few years, though, we've seen the introduction of universal search results that include image and video results. There's neuromarketing research behind this move by the search engines, and it has implications not just for Google and Bing but for every website.

One to One Interactive's OTOinsights unit brought the disparate fields of search engine optimization (SEO) and neuromarketing together by studying how users engaged with SERPs. This research examined the effects of universal search results (which include image and video results) compared with the traditional text-only SERPs.[3]

OTOinsights used eye tracking, biometric monitoring, and questionnaires to gauge user reactions. The findings showed that the universal SERPs did attract the attention of the users and were, in fact, more emotionally engaging.

The media results were located near the top of the search results, and they tended to keep the user's gaze focused on the upper part of the page. Search results and paid ads that were lower on the page garnered less attention when universal results were present. In addition, overall engagement with the search page was higher when the universal results were present.

Brainfluence Takeaway: Add and Optimize Other Media

This research has two main implications for web developers and site owners. First, it's apparent that searchers are attracted to these alternative media and that creating branded and optimized media is a key way of reaching those searchers. It's no longer enough to rely on a top 10 key word ranking in the text results. These media may be on your site, or on specialty media sites like YouTube, but they need to reinforce your message and lead viewers toward your desired goal. Ideally, your content can appear in the image and video results as well as the text listings.

The second implication is more general. If people are more emotionally engaged by search results that have videos and images, it stands to reason that they will engage more with *your* website if appropriate media are present. And, beyond better user engagement, there's a potential rankings benefit, too. Most SEO experts think that sites and pages that incorporate nontext media get a ranking boost in Google's algorithm.

If we combine the idea that on-page media is a positive ranking factor with the findings from the OTOinsights research that universal results are more engaging and more likely to draw clicks, it's clearly time for both SEO experts and marketers to start thinking outside the box— the text box, that is.

95

Reward Versus Reciprocity

MANY OF US work with websites that depend on collecting user information—lead generation sites, charity sites, and so on. Typically, the operators of these sites have content useful to those visitors and want to use that content to encourage visitors to submit their contact data. This valuable content can be provided in a number of forms, such as a white paper, a podcast, a recorded webinar, or a password-protected section of the site.

The most commonly used strategy can be summed up as, "Force visitors to give up their info before we show them the good stuff." But, there's a catch to this approach. If there's an SEO person helping with the site, the immediate objection will be, "You can't put your best content behind a registration form—it won't get indexed by Google or even linked to, and your traffic will tank!"

The good news is that there's a strategy that will keep *both* the SEO experts and the numbers people happy.

Reciprocity Beats Reward

Requiring a user to give up contact data before viewing good content is a *reward* strategy—give us your info, and we'll reward you by letting you see our wonderful stuff. This is an appealing strategy at first glance; 100 percent of the people who use the content will have completed the form, and the valuable information should be a powerful motivator for visitors to comply.

In fact, most users confronted with a form *won't* complete it. If they arrived at the site looking for some specific information, they will likely hit the back button and see if they can get similar data elsewhere without the aggravation of form completion and without the risk of getting unwanted e-mails or phone calls. (Of course, if all the good content is locked away behind a log-in, the number of free visitors arriving by clicking on organic search results will be a lot lower anyway.)

It turns out that a reciprocity strategy can work better; give visitors the info they want and then ask for their information. Italian researchers found that twice as many visitors gave up their contact data if they were able to access the information first. It's counterintuitive, perhaps, but even though these visitors were under no obligation to complete the form, they converted at *double* the rate of visitors seeing the mandatory form.[4]

Not Just for Form Completion

Of course, this approach isn't just for form completion. The psychological principle of reciprocity suggests that visitors who are rewarded in advance would be more likely to buy products, make donations, and so forth. In her book, *Neuro Web Design*, Susan Weinschenk suggests putting a call to action immediately after the good content.

Brainfluence Takeaway: Test the Reciprocity Approach

If you invoke reciprocity, you'll be working with the way our brains are wired and will be more likely to get your visitors to do what you want them to. (And, as an added bonus, your SEO guy will be happy that Google will be able to see your content too!)

As with most aspects of web design, you should test both approaches. It's possible that depending on the perceived value of the content, the simplicity of the sign-up form, and other factors, the reward approach might garner more conversions. But don't assume that the obvious "forced information capture" will automatically capture more leads than relying on visitor goodwill; you might be surprised!

96

Exploit Scarcity on the Fly

E-commerce websites have a great opportunity to exploit the scarcity effect, primarily because they can provide instantaneous feedback on inventory levels and, in a credible way, let customers know when products are scarce.

Merchants use scarcity as part of their call to action in different ways. Amazon knows a few things about e-commerce, and it warns consumers when stock is running low. A typical exhortation that appears as a prominent part of the description is "Only 4 left in stock—order soon." Combine the scarcity effect with, say, one-click ordering and free shipping, and you've got a powerful tool for getting visitors to click the Add to Cart button.

Scarce Seats

Travel is another area that seems to foster indecision. There are often a plethora of flight choices, including dates, times, airports, connections, and intermediate cities. I often have multiple windows open from different travel sites, in each case trying to find the perfect combination of price and convenience.

What's one way to get people to stop dithering? Tell them they might miss their chance to book a flight because the seats are almost gone. Expedia does this with a prominent warning, "1 ticket left at this price," and more than once that was enough to get me to go ahead and book the flight then and there.

Overstock.com—The Scarcity Trifecta

Perhaps the most impressive use of scarcity I've seen is Overstock.com. It has a layered approach that gives consumers several levels of scarcity motivation.

First, Overstock offers a fairly generic warning of low stock on an item. No quantities, but a "sellout" alert, "Sell Out Risk High!" That may be fairly prosaic, but Overstock goes a step further by providing an alert on their search results page that reads, "Almost Sold Out."

On a page featuring many products, I think there's little doubt that the viewer's eye would be drawn to that flagged item. But to complete the scarcity trifecta, Overstock has one more card to play: it keeps sold-out items in their results and flags them as "Sold Out."

Some might find that a risky move—showing customers an unavailable but interesting product might cause them to try to find it elsewhere. Or customers might decide to buy nothing at all if an attractive product was sold out. Nevertheless, these "Sold Out" indicators add credibility to the other scarcity warnings and add a sense of urgency to the shopping process.

Daily Scarcity

The explosive growth of daily deal sites like Groupon are in part scarcity-based. They combine short-duration offers (typically 24 hours) with limits on how many offers will be sold to encourage consumers to act immediately.

Recently, I've been receiving e-mail sale notifications from e-commerce fashion merchant RueLaLa.com. It, too, exploits scarcity. Rue La La sales last only 24 hours, and, like Overstock, sold-out merchandise is left on the site, although it is pushed to the end of the listings and flagged as no longer available. This combination builds urgency into the ordering process.

Brainfluence Takeaway: Use Scarcity and Be Specific

The best way to imply scarcity in a credible way is to be specific. Tell visitors to the site how many you have left, if your technology lets you do that. "Only 2 left at this price" is much better than "Limited supply." If the volume of your offering is such that your inventory changes often, a dynamic display of scarcity would be even better. I think a really effective message would be something like, "Just sold another! Only 1 left!"

That may not work for every e-commerce site, but just about all sites can boost sales using at least one variation of the scarcity effect.

97

Target Boomers With Simplicity

IF YOU ARE marketing to baby boomers or seniors with your advertising, here's one key: *keep it simple*. Although that's usually good advice for any kind of advertising, brain scans show a dramatic difference in the ability of older brains to suppress distracting information. Studies by Dr. Adam

Gazzaley showed that the suppression difference in older versus younger brains was the key factor in memory formation decline in older people.

Using fMRI scans to examine younger and older adult brains during memory tasks, Gazzaley found that both young and old brains were able to activate their brains effectively for building memories but the older brains were far worse at suppressing irrelevant information. (A similar study using EEG, still under review, suggests that the difference in suppression is due to a decline in neural processing speed.[5])

The latest research by Gazzaley shows that the lower performance of older brains when multitasking is a switching glitch—in essence, when distracted, the older brains switched from the memory task to processing the interruption, and the memory was less likely to be stored.[6]

Brainfluence Takeaway: Keep It Simple

In *The Buying Brain*, A. K. Pradeep cites Gazzaley's research and suggests these tactics for marketers hoping to appeal to baby boomers and seniors:

- Keep the message obvious.
- Use an uncluttered layout for copy and images.
- Include some white space around the message.
- Avoid distractions like running screens, sounds, and animations.

Simplicity is an ongoing theme of mine; a simple approach seems to work best in many situations, whether it's choosing a simple font or using a simple guarantee. As a general rule, I recommend striving for simplicity. Even younger brains will do a better job of processing your message!

98

Use Your Customer's Imagination

IN A PREVIOUS chapter, I described a study by marketing professors Joann Peck and Suzanne Shu that focused on how touching an object increased feelings of ownership (see page 231). An additional finding in that study has implications for selling online. Even when customers can't touch a product, it is still possible to increase their perceived ownership using what Peck and Shu term ownership imagery.

They asked the subjects in the study questions such as, "Imagine taking the product home with you. Where would you keep it? What would you do with it?" The duration of the imagery session was a mere 60 seconds. Although it was true that the imagery had an impact on the feeling of ownership, there was a bigger surprise in the data: even when no touching was involved, the subjects exposed to ownership imagery were still influenced.

Peck and Shu conclude, "Online retailers who can encourage ownership imagery among potential buyers may be able to increase both perceived ownership and valuation. In the no-touch environment, ownership imagery was powerful in increasing both the feeling of ownership and the amount a consumer was willing to pay."

Brainfluence Takeaway: Help Customers Imagine Ownership

If you can help your customers imagine that they own the product, your chances of making a sale increase. The question, naturally, is how to do that within the confines of a website or mobile application.

One simple, low-cost way to do this would be to ask leading questions in the product's copy, much as experimenters did in person. Of course, unlike the in-person research condition, you have little control over your customers or the time they spend on any given activity. In addition, on a site with many products, visualization instructions on each one might seem a bit bizarre.

Still, in some e-commerce situations, the copy might be effective. Some Internet marketers use a squeeze page for a single product—one long page filled with product data, testimonials from satisfied customers, answers to common objections, and so on. Typically, the customer who makes it well into the page is quite engaged and might be open to ownership imagery.

One of the best ownership imagery examples I've seen online is at TireRack.com, a national seller of auto tires and wheels. Customers begin the selection process by specifying the make, model, and year of their car. The site then brings up a selection of appropriate wheels and tires. Once the customer sees, say, a set of wheels that are of interest, he or she clicks "View on Vehicle." A picture of the customer's exact vehicle appears, with a drop-down box listing the manufacturer's colors for that model. The user selects the correct color, and presto—the customer sees his or her very own vehicle rendered beautifully with the wheels and tires just picked out.

For some sites, it might be relevant to include a video that, along with a discussion of product features, included ownership imagery prompts. Every site is different, but finding a way to build a sense of perceived ownership will increase the conversion rate and total revenue.

99

Avoid the Corner of Death

WHAT'S THE WORST place to put your logo, and where do advertisers most often put their logo in print ads, TV spots, and direct-mail pieces? The answer is the same: the lower right corner, an area dubbed the corner of death by facial coding expert Dan Hill.[7] Hill's comments stem from an interesting eye-tracking study by Steve Outing and Laura Rule.[8]

In a recent article, Hill says that the lower right corner is the second to last place people look. Many may not get that far if they are processing the page quickly or aren't engaged by the content they view first.

Despite these findings, the lower right corner is by far the most common single location for the primary logo/brand identity use in all types of advertising, according to Hill.

Brainfluence Takeaway: Put Your Brand Front and Center

Based on eye-tracking research, where *should* the logo or brand identity be placed so that consumers actually see it? Hill says that the best place is the lower middle part of the page or layout, At that point, the viewer will have engaged emotionally with the leading part of the ad and will then have the opportunity to associate the brand with solving a problem or satisfying consumers' wants.

100

Computers as People

FORGET THE TURING test! (That test, proposed in 1950, was a measure of machine intelligence that required a machine to interact with a person so effectively that the person could not distinguish it from a human.) But you don't have to try to fool people; research shows well-designed automation can make people feel like they are interacting with a real person even when they know they aren't.

So, what can businesses do to make computer interactions more "human"? It turns out that people *do* tend to treat computers like people and that changing the interaction can enhance that tendency. Here are a few ways to humanize your automation.

Get on the Same Team

It's well established that people will form team allegiances very quickly and with very little prompting. Studies show that people can bond with computers in much the same way. Stanford University professor Clifford Nass arbitrarily divided subjects into two groups. Half were told they were on the blue team and wore a blue wristband while working on a blue-bordered monitor. The other half used a green-bordered monitor and were told that they were a blue person working with the green computer.

Even though there was no difference in the details of the human-computer interaction between the two groups, the participants who were told they were on a team rated their computer as smarter and more helpful. They also worked harder, apparently because of the "bond" formed with their computer.[9]

Can you find some common ground with your users? Do you have some individual user data that would let you, say, tailor an interface to each user? (One trivial example: if you know a user's favorite sports team, you could embellish the interface with that team's colors.)

Nass posits that one can use just about every social science finding about people-to-people interactions and apply it to people and computers.

"I'm on *Your* Side!"

One of the most reviled computer characters in PC history was Microsoft's Clippy, a cartoon paper clip that seemed to delight in asking users inane and repetitive questions about what they were doing in a (usually) vain attempt to help. Clippy was so annoying that hate sites, fan groups, and videos targeting him sprang up around the web. Nass found that all this emotion could be negated easily.

He and his team re-created a Clippy that made it sound like Clippy was on the user's side by saying things like, "That gets me really angry! Let's tell Microsoft how bad their help system is." If a user created a complaint e-mail, Clippy would provide added encouragement: "C'mon! You can be tougher than that. Let 'em have it!"

These changes turned Clippy-haters into Clippy-lovers. Every user in the test liked Clippy, with one exclaiming, "He's so supportive!"

Got a feedback function? Like Clippy 2.0, position the interface as being on the user's side, not yours. (Good human salespeople know this works. When things go wrong with an order, they position themselves as customer advocates rather than company apologists.)

Specialized = Smart

People accord more wisdom to devices that specialize. Nass found that people rated TV news programs more highly on multiple criteria when they thought the TV they were watching showed only news content.

Making your computer interface "an expert" will increase its credibility. People will trust a "Business Laptop Configuration Wizard" more than an "Order Form."

Brainfluence Takeaway: It's Not a Computer; It's a Person!

If you are going to structure a human-computer interaction, assume that people will think of the computer as a person! That means incorporating the right social strategy: imagine that you were trying to train a new (and slightly dense) employee how to interact emotionally with the customer and build that logic into the automated system.

The three approaches outlined, either individually or in combination, will dramatically improve the way your customers feel about your automated processes.

Afterword

What's Next?

I'M EXCITED ABOUT the future of marketing, advertising, and branding. Without losing the art of these disciplines, we are on the threshold of adding the missing science.

Everyone involved in marketing has seen bad decisions that led to failed products and ineffective campaigns. Some of these were predictable, like a train chugging toward a collapsed bridge. Others appeared to be promising to all involved, but then were rejected by seemingly fickle customers. Resources were squandered, careers were derailed, and in some cases, the companies themselves foundered.

Neuromarketing techniques are no panacea for marketing failure, but in some cases, they can identify problem products and ineffective ads before they are launched at great expense. More importantly, perhaps, they can provide objective support to those marketers who really do understand their customers but who aren't the ultimate decision makers.

Although I expect neuromarketing studies using brain analytics and biometrics to become increasingly affordable, not every project will be able to justify that type of approach. Even in those cases, though, behavioral studies and more general neuroscience and neuroeconomics work can inform marketing decisions.

That's the point of this book—know how our brains work, and you'll have better products and better marketing. And the best is yet to come!

Endnotes

Chapter 1

1. Gerald Zaltman, *How Customers Think* (Boston: Harvard Business School Press, 2003).

2. A. K. Pradeep, *The Buying Brain: Secrets for Selling to the Subconscious Mind* (Hoboken, NJ: John Wiley & Sons, 2010), 4.

3. "Incognito: Evidence Mounts That Brains Decide Before Their Owners Know About It," *Economist* 390, no. 8627 (April 18, 2009): 86–87, http://www.economist.com/node/13489722?story_id=13489722.

Section 1: Price and Product Brainfluence

1. Brian Knutson et al., "Neural Predictors of Purchases," *Neuron* 53, no.1 (January 4, 2007): 147–156, http://www.neuron.org/content/article/abstract?uid=PIIS0896627306009044.

2. Richard Thaler, "Transaction Utility Theory," *Advances in Consumer Research* 10 (1983): 229–232.

3. Lisa Scherzer, "Professor: Pain, Not Logic, Dictates Spending," *SmartMoney*, March 22, 2007, http://www.smartmoney.com/invest/markets/professor-pain-not-logic-dictates-spending-20987/.

4. Sybil S. Yang, Sheryl E. Kimes, and Mauro M. Sessarego, "$ or Dollars: Effects of Menu-price Formats on Restaurant Checks," *Cornell Hospitality Reports* 9, no. 8,

The Center for Hospitality Research, Cornell University School of Hotel Administration, http://www.hotelschool.cornell.edu/research/chr/pubs/reports/abstract-15048.html.

5. Dan Ariely, *Predictably Irrational: The Hidden Forces That Shape Our Decisions*, rev. ed. (New York: Harper Perennial, 2010).

6. Lisa Trei, "Price Changes Way People Experience Wine," *Stanford News Service*, January 16, 2008, http://news.stanford.edu/news/2008/january16/wine-011608.html.

7. Benedict Carey, "More Expensive Placebos Bring More Relief," *New York Times*, March 5, 2008, http://www.nytimes.com/2008/03/05/health/research/05placebo.html.

8. Wray Herbert, "Why Things Cost $19.95," *Scientific American Mind* 19, no. 2 (April 2008), http://www.scientificamerican.com/article.cfm?id=why-thin,gs-cost-1995&ec=su_1995.

9. Ibid.

10. Ariely, *Predictably Irrational*.

11. University of Minnesota, "Inside the Consumer Mind: U of M Brain Scans Reveal Choice Mechanism," news release, December 11, 2008, http://www.eurekalert.org/pub_releases/2008-12/uom-itc121108.php.

12. Barbara Buell, "The Limits of One-to-One Marketing," *Stanford Business* 68, no. 4 (August 2000), http://www.gsb.stanford.edu/community/bmag/sbsm0008/faculty_research_mktg.html.

13. Itamar Simonson, "The Effect of Product Assortment on Buyer Preferences," *Journal of Retailing* 75, no. 3 (Autumn 1999): 347–370, http://www.sciencedirect.com/science/article/pii/S0022435999000123.

14. Sheena S. Iyengar and Mark R. Lepper, "When Choice Is Demotivating: Can One Desire Too Much of a Good Thing?" *Journal of Personality and Social Psychology* 79, no. 6 (December 2000): 995–1006, http://psycnet.apa.org/?&fa=main.doiLanding&doi=10.1037/0022-3514.79.6.995.

15. Randy Dotinga, "Choices Sap Your Stamina, Self Control," *Washington Post*, April 18, 2008, http://www.washingtonpost.com/wp-dyn/content/article/2008/04/18/AR2008041802473.html.

16. Ned Augenblick and Scott Nicholson, "Choice Fatigue: The Effect of Making Previous Choices on Decision Making in a Voting Context," Haas School of Business, University of California, Berkeley (February 2011): 1–29, http://faculty.haas.berkeley.edu/ned/Choice_Fatigue.pdf.

17. Marina Strauss, "In Store Aisles, Less Is More but Customers Can Still Be Particular," *Globe and Mail*, May 18, 2010, http://www.theglobeandmail.com/report-on-business/in-store-aisles-less-is-more-but-customers-can-still-be-particular/article1573518/.

Section 2: Sensory Brainfluence

1. Laird, D. (1935). What can you do with your nose? Scientific Monthly. 41: 126-30

2. "Clubbers Can Smell a Good Nightspot," *ScienceDaily*, May 17, 2011, http://www.sciencedaily.com/releases/2011/05/110517105141.htm.

3. Kate Fox, "The Smell Report," Social Issues Research Centre, http://www.sirc.org/publik/smell.pdf.

4. Nicholas Bakalar, "Varying Sweat Scents Are Noted by Women," *New York Times*, February 16, 2009, http://www.nytimes.com/2009/02/17/health/17swea.html.

5. "N.Y. grocery turns to scent marketing." CBSNews.com. 13 Aug. 2011. CBS News. 18 July 2011; www.cbsnews.com/stories/2011/07/18/earlyshow/main20080320.shtml.

6. *Neuromarketing*; "Sensory Marketing to Jolt Espresso Sales," in *Neuromarketing*, a blog by Roger Dooley, November 1, 2007, http://www.neurosciencemarketing.com/blog/articles/espresso-sensory-selling.htm.

7. Adrian C. North, David J. Hargreaves, and Jennifer Mckendrick, "Music and On-hold Waiting Time," *British Journal of Psychology* 90, no. 1 (February 1999): 161–164, http://onlinelibrary.wiley.com/doi/10.1348/000712699161215/abstract; Adrian C. North and David J. Hargreaves, "The Effects of Musical Complexity and Silence on Waiting Time," *Environment and Behavior* 31, no. 1 (January 1999): 136–149, http://eab.sagepub.com/content/31/1/136.

8. Susan Hallam and John Price, "Can the Use of Background Music Improve the Behavior and Academic Performance of Children with Emotional and Behavioural Difficulties?" *British Journal of Special Education* 25, no. 2 (June 1998): 88–91, http://onlinelibrary.wiley.com/doi/10.1111/1467-8527.t01-1-00063/abstract.

9. Adrian C. North and David J. Hargreaves, "The Effects of Music on Atmosphere in a Bank and a Bar," *Journal of Applied Social Psychology* 30, no. 7 (June 2000): 1504–1522, http://onlinelibrary.wiley.com/doi/10.1111/j.1559-1816.2000.tb02533.x/abstract.

10. John Medina, *Brain Rules: 12 Principles for Surviving and Thriving at Work, Home, and School* (Seattle: Pear Press, 2008).

11. Reuters, "Candidate Secretly Sniffs Out Voters," December 13, 2007, http://uk.reuters.com/article/2007/12/13/oukoe-uk-korea-election-perfume-idUKSEO1534820071213?feedType=RSS&feedName=oddlyEnoughNews.

12. *Journal of Consumer Research*, "Does Scent Enhance Product Memories?" news release, December 14, 2009, https://www.jcr-admin.org/files/pressreleases/121409105836Krishnarelease.pdf.

13. "Early Scents Really Do Get 'Etched' in the Brain," *ScienceDaily*, November 6, 2009, http://www.sciencedaily.com/releases/2009/11/091105132448.htm.

14. Ideair, "Sell Better with Scents," http://www.ideair.fi/sales.html.

15. Pradeep, *The Buying Brain*.

Section 3: Brainfluence Branding

1. Radiological Society of North America, "MRI Shows Brains Respond Better to Name Brands," news release, November 28, 2006, http://www.eurekalert.org/pub_releases/2006-11/rson-msb112106.php.

2. Edwin Colyer, "The Science of Branding," *BrandChannel*, March 15, 2004, http://www.brandchannel.com/features_effect.asp?pf_id=20.1.

3. Norman Doidge, *The Brain That Changes Itself: Stories of Personal Triumph from the Frontiers of Brain Science* (New York: Penguin Group, 2007).

4. Shaoni Bhattacharya, "How Brands Get Wired Into the Brain," *NewScientist*, January 4, 2006, http://www.newscientist.com/article/dn8535.

5. Heath, R. (1999) "The Low-Involvement Processing Theory," Admap 34 (March): 14–17]

6. Jeremy Hsu, "TV Ads Grab Attention in Fast-Forward," *Live Science*, October 2, 2008, http://www.livescience.com/2931-tv-ads-grab-attention-fast.html.

7. Benedict Carey, "Blind, Yet Seeing: The Brain's Subconscious Visual Sense," *New York Times*, December 22, 2008, http://www.nytimes.com/2008/12/23/health/23blin.html?_r=2.

8. Robert B. Zajonc, "Attitudinal Effects of Mere Exposure," *Journal of Personality and Social Psychology* 9, no. 2, pt. 2 (June 1968): 1–27, http://psycnet.apa.org/?&fa=main.doiLanding&doi=10.1037/h0025848.

9. Kate Newlin, *Passion Brands: Why Some Brands Are Just Gotta Have, Drive All Night For, and Tell All Your Friends About* (Amherst, NY: Prometheus Books, 2009).

10. Alex Riley and Adam Boome, "Superbrands' Success Fuelled by Sex, Religion and Gossip," BBC News, May 16, 2011, http://www.bbc.co.uk/news/business-13416598.

11. Henri Tajfel et al., "Social Categorization and Intergroup Behaviour," *European Journal of Social Psychology* 1, no. 2 (April–June 1971): 149–178, http://sozpsy .sowi.uni-mannheim.de/intranet/php/lecture/files/Tajfel_Billig_Bundy_ Flament_1971_EJSP.pdf.

12. *Seth Godin's Blog;* "Tribe Management," in *Seth Godin's Blog,* January 30, 2008, http://sethgodin.typepad.com/seths_blog/2008/01/tribal-manageme.html.

13. "Why Some Americans Believe Obama Is a Muslim," *ScienceDaily,* August 31, 2010, http://www.sciencedaily.com/releases/2010/08/100831102828.htm.

Section 4: Brainfluence in Print

1. "Using Neuroscience to Understand the Role of Direct Mail," Millward Brown Case Study, 2009, http://www.millwardbrown.com/Insights/CaseStudies/ NeuroscienceDirectMail.aspx.

2. *Journal of Consumer Research,* "Faking It: Can Ads Create False Memories About Products?" news release, May 9, 2011, http://www.jcr-admin.org/files/press- releases/050811130432_Rajagopalrelease.pdf.

3. Joshua M. Ackerman, Christopher C. Nocera, and John A. Bargh, "Incidental Haptic Sensations Influence Social Judgments and Decisions," *Science* 328, no. 5986 (June 25, 2010): 1712–1715, http://www.sciencemag.org/content/328/5986/1712.

4. Hyunjin Song and Norbert Schwarz, "If It's Hard to Read, It's Hard to Do: Processing Fluency Affects Effort Prediction and Motivation," *Psychological Science* 19, no. 10 (October 2008): 986–988, http://sitemaker.umich.edu/norbert. schwarz/files/08_ps_song___schwarz_effort.pdf.

5. Ibid.

6. Connor Diemand-Yauman, Daniel M. Oppenheimer, and Erikka B. Vaughan, "Fortune Favors the Bold (and the Italicized): Effects of Disfluency on Educational Outcomes, *Cognition* 188, no. 1 (January 2011): 111–115, http://web.princeton .edu/sites/opplab/papers/Diemand-Yauman_Oppenheimer_2010.pdf.

Section 5: Picture Brainfluence

1. Morten L. Kringelbach et al., "A Specific and Rapid Neural Signature for Parental Instinct," *Plos One,* February 27, 2008, http://www.plosone.org/article/ info:doi%2F10.1371%2Fjournal.pone.0001664.

2. *UsableWorld;* "You Look Where They Look," in *UsableWorld,* a blog by James Breeze, March 16, 2009, http://usableworld.com.au/2009/03/16/you-look-where-they-look/.

3. Marianne Bertrand et al., "What's Psychology Worth? A Field Experiment in the Consumer Credit Market," research at Princeton, October 31, 2005, http://www.princeton.edu/rpds/papers/pdfs/Shafir_2006Whats%20Psych%20Worth_%20South%20Africa.pdf.

4. Brian Alexander, "Science Proves That Bikinis Turn Men into Boobs," MSNBC, June 20, 2008, http://www.msnbc.msn.com/id/25197962/.

5. Ibid.

6. David Eagleman, *Incognito: The Secret Lives of the Brain* (New York: Pantheon, 2011).

7. Radiological Society of North America, "Patient Photos Spur Radiologist Empathy and Eye for Detail," news release, December 2, 2008, http://www.rsna.org/media/pressreleases/pr_target.cfm?ID=389.

Section 6: Loyalty and Trust Brainflulence

1. Hal Ersner-Hershfield et al., "Company, Country, Connections: Counterfactual Origins Increase Organizational Commitment, Patriotism, and Social Investment," *Psychological Science* 21, no. 10 (October 2010): 1479–1486, http://www.kellogg.northwestern.edu/?sc_itemid={CFCFA812-F244-4E6E-BE1C-387FF7E5A04C}.

2. Minkyung Koo et al., "It's a Wonderful Life: Mentally Subtracting Positive Events Improves People's Affective States, Contrary to Their Affective Forecasts," *Journal of Personality and Social Psychology* 95, no. 5 (November 2008): 1217–1224, http://www.ncbi.nlm.nih.gov/pmc/articles/PMC2746912/.

3. Jochen Wirtz, Anna S. Mattila, and May Oo Lwin, "How Effective Are Loyalty Reward Programs in Driving Share of Wallet?" *Journal of Service Research* 9, no. 4 (May 2007): 327–334, http://www.sagepub.com/clow/study/articles/PDFs/14_WIrtz.pdf.

4. Stijn M. J. Van Osselaer, Joseph W. Alba, and Puneet Manchanda, "Irrelevant Information and Mediated Intertemporal Choice," *Journal of Consumer Psychology* 14, no. 3 (June 2004): 257–270, http://www-personal.umich.edu/~pmanchan/Published_files/Van-osselaer_Alba_Manchanda_JCP_2004.pdf.

5. Ran Kivetz, Oleg Urminsky, and Yuhuang Zheng, "The Goal-Gradient Hypothesis Resurrected: Purchase Acceleration, Illusionary Goal Progress, and Customer

Retention," *Journal of Marketing Research* 43 (February 2006): 39–58, http://www .columbia.edu/~rk566/research/Goal-Gradient_Illusionary_Goal_Progress.pdf.

6. Ori Brafman and Rom Brafman, *Sway: The Irresistible Pull of Irrational Behavior* (New York: Doubleday, 2008).

7. Malcolm Gladwell, *Blink: The Power of Thinking Without Thinking* (New York: Little, Brown, 2005).

8. Fuan Li and Paul W. Miniard, "On the Potential for Advertising to Facilitate Trust in the Advertised Brand," *Journal of Advertising* 35, no. 4 (Winter 2006): 101–112, http://mesharpe.metapress.com/app/home/contribution.asp?referrer=parent& backto=issue,8,12;journal,18,33;linkingpublicationresults,1:110658,1.

9. *The Moral Molecule*; "How to Run a Con," in *The Moral Molecule*, a blog by Paul J. Zak, November 13, 2008, http://www.psychologytoday.com/blog/ the-moral-molecule/200811/how-run-con.

Section 7: Brainfluence in Person

1. Kay-Yut Chen and Marina Krakovsky, *Secrets of the Moneylab: How Behavioral Economics Can Improve Your Business* (New York: Portfolio Penguin, 2010).

2. C. H. Loch and Y. Wu, "Social Preferences and Supply Chain Performance: An Experimental Study," *Management Science* 54, no. 11 (2008), 1835–1849.

3. Richard Alleyne, "Handshake Key to Landing a Job, Scientists Claim," *The Telegraph*, September 26, 2008, http://www.telegraph.co.uk/news/3085731/ Handshake-key-to-landing-a-job-scientists-claim.html.

4. Paul J. Zak, "The Power of a Handshake: How Touch Sustains Personal and Business Relationships," *HuffPost Business*, September 29, 2008, http://www .huffingtonpost.com/paul-j-zak/the-power-of-a-handshake_b_129441.html.

5. Columbia Business School, "A Touch of Risk," *Ideas@work*, March 26, 2010, http:// www4.gsb.columbia.edu/ideasatwork/feature/7211685/A+Touch+of+Risk.

6. "Need Something? Talk To My Right Ear," *ScienceDaily*, June 23, 2009, http:// www.sciencedaily.com/releases/2009/06/090623090705.htm.

7. Piotr Winkielman and Kent C. Berridge, "Unconscious Emotion," *Current Directions in Psychological Science* 13, no. 3 (June 2004): 120–123, http://psy2.ucsd .edu/~pwinkiel/winkielman-berridge_Unconscious_Emotion_CDIPS-2004.pdf.

8. Peter Aldhous, "Humans Prefer Cockiness to Expertise," *New Scientist* 202, no. 2711 (June 3, 2009): 15, http://www.newscientist.com/article/mg20227115.500- humans-prefer-cockiness-to-expertise.html.

9. Ker Than, "Scientists Say Everyone Can Read Minds," *Live Science*, April 27, 2005, http://www.livescience.com/220-scientists-read-minds.html.

10. Robert Cialdini, Noah Goldsten, and Steve Martin, *Yes! 50 Scientifically Proven Ways to Be Persuasive* (New York: Free Press, 2008).

11. Ibid.

12. Nicole Branan, "Ability to Guess Others' Thoughts Tied to Language Proficiency," *Scientific American Mind* 20, no. 6 (November 2009): 8, http://www.scientific american.com/article.cfm?id=language-skills-and-reading-minds.

13. John Tierney, "Heart-Warming News on Hot Coffee," *New York Times*, October 23, 2008, http://tierneylab.blogs.nytimes.com/2008/10/23/heart-warming-news-on-coffee/.

14. "Caffeine Boosts Brain's Short-Term Memory Function," Daily News Central, December 1, 2005, http://health.dailynewscentral.com/content/view/0001975/62/.

15. University of Miami School of Business Administration, "School of Business Research Shows One Tiny Chocolate May Cause Overindulgent Eating & Shopping," news release, February 10, 2009, http://www.bus.miami.edu/news-and-media/recent-news/truffles-research.html.

16. Stephen L. Macknik, Susana Martinez-Conde, and Sandra Blakeslee, *Sleights of Mind: What the Neuroscience of Magic Reveals About Our Everyday Deceptions* (New York: Henry Holt, 2010).

17. Joshua M. Ackerman, Christopher C. Nocera, and John A. Bargh, "Incidental Haptic Sensations Influence Social Judgments and Decisions," *Science* 328, no. 5986 (June 25, 2010): 1712–1715, http://www.sciencemag.org/content/328/5986/1712.

Section 8: Brainfluence for a Cause

1. Robert Cialdini, Noah Goldsten, and Steve Martin, *Yes! 50 Scientifically Proven Ways to Be Persuasive* (New York: Free Press, 2008).

2. Lawrence J. Sanna et al., "Rising Up to Higher Virtues: Experiencing Elevated Physical Height Uplifts Prosocial Actions," *Journal of Experimental Social Psychology* 47 (2011): 472–476, http://www-personal.umich.edu/~ljsanna/ljs11jesp.pdf.

3. Hannah Devlin, "Want to keep your wallet? Carry a baby picture," *The Times*, July 11, 2009, http://www.timesonline.co.uk/tol/news/science/article 6681923.ece.

4. Armin Falk, "Charitable Giving as a Gift Exchange: Evidence from a Field Experiment," Institute of the Study of Labor, Discussion Paper 1148, May 2004, http://ftp.iza.org/dp1148.pdf.

5. Clive Thompson, "Clive Thompson Explains Why We Can Count on Geeks to Rescue the Earth," *Wired Magazine*, August 21, 2007, http://www.wired.com/techbiz/people/magazine/15-09/st_thompson.

6. Aaron C. Kay, S. Christian Wheeler, John A. Bargh, and Lee Ross, "Material Priming: The Influence of Mundane Physical Objects on Situational Construal and Competitive Behavioral Choice," *Organizational Behavior and Human Decision Processes* 95, issue 1 (2004):83–96.

7. David Rivers, "How to Win More Sales: 5 Lessons I Learned From the Best Selling Girl Scout in America," *Success*, December 23, 2008, http://www.successmagazine .com/article/print?articleId=509.

Section 9: Brainfluence Copywriting

1. "Tales of the Unexpected: How the Brain Detects Novelty," *Medical News Today*, November 30, 2006, http://www.medicalnewstoday.com/releases/57648.php.

2. "Scientists Watch as Listener's Brain Predicts Speaker's Words," *Science-Daily*, September 15, 2008, http://www.sciencedaily.com/releases/2008/09/080911140815.htm.

3. Steve Mirsky, "Listener Anticipates Speaker's Word Choice," *Scientific American*, podcast audio, September 12, 2008, http://www.scientificamerican.com/podcast/episode.cfm?id=56B932C3-0722-2562-5F1275228E5F3714.

4. http://moya.bus.miami.edu/~jularan/Papers/PE_LaranDaltonAndrade_JCR.pdf?

5. Armen Hareyan, "Reading Shakespeare May Have Dramatic Effect on Human Brain," *EmaxHealth*, January 30, 2007, http://www.emaxhealth.com/7/9254.html.

6. Caglar Irmak, Beth Vallen, and Stefanie Rosen Robinson, "The Impact of Product Name on Dieters' and Nondieters' Food Evaluations and Consumption," *Journal of Consumer Research*, April 12, 2011, http://www.jstor.org/stable/10.1086/660044.

7. Jason Zweig, *Your Money and Your Brain: How the New Science of Neuroeconomics Can Help Make You Rich* (New York: Simon and Schuster, 2007).

8. Roger Highfield, "'Sense of Adventure' Makes Us Marketing Targets," *The Telegraph*, June 25, 2008, http://www.telegraph.co.uk/science/science-news/3345444/Sense-of-adventure-makes-us-marketing-targets.html.

9. Sarah Kershaw, "Using Menu Psychology to Entice Diners," *New York Times,* December 22, 2009, http://www.nytimes.com/2009/12/23/dining/23menus .html.

10. *We're Only Human;* "The Narrative in the Neurons," in *We're Only Human,* a blog by Wray Herbert, July 14, 2009, http://www.psychologicalscience.org/only human/2009/07/narrative-in-neurons.cfm.

11. Greg J. Stephens, Lauren J. Silbert, and Uri Hasson, "Speaker–Listener Neural Coupling Underlies Successful Communication," *Proceedings of the National Academy of Sciences of the United States of America* 107, no. 32 (August 10, 2010): 14425–14430, http://www.pnas.org/content/107/32/14425.full.pdf+html?sid= af1e1664-a040-42d0-9f79-bf44eedbc1af.

12. Christopher Chabris and Daniel Simons, *The Invisible Gorilla: And Other Ways Our Intuitions Deceive Us* (New York: Crown, 2010).

13. "Parisian Love," YouTube video, 00:52, uploaded by SearchStories, November 19, 2009, http://www.youtube.com/watch?v=nnsSUqgkDwU.

14. Michigan State University, "MSU Profs Rate Google Ad Top Super Bowl Commercial," news release, February 7, 2010, http://news.msu.edu/story/7416.

15. *Neuromarketing;* "Super Bowl 2010 Ad Winners," in *Neuromarketing,* a blog by Roger Dooley, February 24, 2010, http://www.neurosciencemarketing.com/ blog/articles/super-bowl-2010-ad-winners.htm.

Section 10: Consumer Brainfluence

1. S. Alexander Haslam, "I Think, Therefore I Err," *Scientific American Mind* 18, no. 2 (April 2007): 16–17, http://www.scientificamerican.com/article.cfm?id=i-think- therefore-i-err.

2. "Sleep on It, Decision-Makers Told," BBC News, February 17, 2006, http:// news.bbc.co.uk/2/hi/health/4723216.stm.

3. Irving Biederman and Edward Vessel, "Perceptual Pleasure and the Brain," *American Scientist* 94, no. 3 (May–June 2006): 247, http://condition.org/ as65-6.htm.

4. Sarah Jane Gilbert, "Understanding the 'Want' vs. 'Should' Decision," Harvard Business School, July 16, 2007, http://hbswk.hbs.edu/item/5693.html.

5. Todd Rogers, Katherine L. Milkman, and Max H. Bazerman, "I'll Have the Ice Cream Soon and the Vegetables Later: Decreasing Impatience Over Time in

Online Grocery Orders," Harvard Business School, May 15, 2007, http://www
.hbs.edu/research/pdf/07-078.pdf.

6. Scott I. Rick, Cynthia E. Cryder, and George Loewenstein, "Tightwads and
Spendthrifts," Knowledge@Wharton, September 1, 2007, http://knowledge
.wharton.upenn.edu/papers/1342.pdf.

7. Jason Zweig, "Your money and your brain," CNNMoney, August 23, 2007, http://
money.cnn.com/2007/08/14/pf/zweig.moneymag/?postversion=2007082313.

8. Gordon T. Anderson, "Pepsi's Billion-Dollar Monkey," *CNNMoney*, May 2, 2003,
http://money.cnn.com/2003/04/09/news/companies/pepsi_billion_game/
index.htm.

9. Sharon Begley, "A, My Name is Alice: Moniker Madness," *Newsweek*, November
7, 2007, http://www.newsweek.com/blogs/lab-notes/2007/11/07/a-my-name-
is-alice-moniker-madness.html.

10. Brett W. Pelham, Matthew C. Mirenberg, and John T. Jones, "Why Susie Sells
Seashells by the Seashore: Implicit Egotism and Major Life Decisions," *Journal
of Personality and Social Psychology* 82, no. 4 (2002): 469–487, http://www.stat
.columbia.edu/~gelman/stuff_for_blog/susie.pdf.

11. John F. Finch and Robert B. Cialdini, "Another Indirect Tactic of (Self-) Image
Management," *Personality and Social Psychology Bulletin* 15, no. 2 (June 1989): 222–232,
http://psp.sagepub.com/content/15/2/222.abstract.

12. Lisa Trei, "Price Changes Way People Experience Wine," *Stanford News Service*,
January 16, 2008, http://news.stanford.edu/news/2008/january16/wine-
011608.html.

13. Cornell University, "Fine as North Dakota Wine," news release, August 6, 2007,
http://www.eurekalert.org/pub_releases/2007-08/cfb-fan080607.php.

14. Paul McDougall, "Microsoft Dupes Windows Vista Haters with 'Mojave
Experiment'," *Information Week*, July 29, 2008, http://www.informationweek
.com/news/windows/operatingsystems/209800457.

15. Susan Ager, "A dime can make a difference," *Baltimore Sun*, August 22, 1999, http://
articles.baltimoresun.com/1999-08-22/news/9908240363_1_schwarz-dime-life.

Section 11: Gender Brainfluence

1. Ronald Kotulak, "Hormones Wire Men's, Women's Brains Differently,"
Baltimore Sun, May 19, 2006, http://articles.baltimoresun.com/2006-05-19/
news/0605190009_1_hormones-female-or-male-puberty.

2. "Blatant Benevolence and Conspicuous Consumption," *Economist* 384, no. 8540 (August 4, 2007): 67–68, http://www.economist.com/node/9581656?story_id=9581656.

3. Wendy Leopold, "Gender Differences in Languages Appear Biological," Northwestern University, March 11, 2008, http://www.northwestern.edu/news center/stories/2008/03/burmangender.html.

4. Douglas D. Burman, Tali Bitan, and James R. Booth, "Sex Differences in Neural Processing of Language Among Children," *Neuropsychologia* 46, no. 5 (2008): 1349–1362, http://www.sciencedirect.com/science/article/pii/S0028393207004460.

5. Marion Luna Brem, *Women Make the Best Salesmen: Isn't It Time You Started Using their Secrets?* (New York: Doubleday, 2004).

6. Margo Wilson and Martin Daly, "Do Pretty Women Inspire Men to Discount the Future?" *Proceedings of the Royal Society* 271, Suppl. 4 (May 2004): S177–S179, http://rspb.royalsocietypublishing.org/content/271/Suppl_4/S177.full.pdf.

7. Lei Chang, Hui Jing Lu, Hongli Li, and Tong Li, Pers Soc Psychol Bull, July 2011; vol. 37, 7: pp. 976–984, first published on March 23, 2011.

Section 12: Shopper Brainfluence

1. Laura Brinn, "When Cookies Catch the Cooties," *Duke Today*, April 30, 2007, http://today.duke.edu/2007/04/cooties.html.

2. "The Retail Consumer Report: Bring Back Unhappy Customers via Social Media," Right Now (2011): 1–6, http://www.rightnow.com/files/Retail-Consumer-Report.pdf.

3. Joann Peck and Suzanne B. Shu, "The Effect of Mere Touch on Perceived Ownership," *Journal of Consumer Research*, October 2009.

4. Elliot Aronson and Judson Mills, "The Effect of Severity of Initiation on Liking for a Group," http://faculty.uncfsu.edu/tvancantfort/Syllabi/Gresearch/Readings/A_Aronson.pdf.

Section 13: Video, TV, and Film Brainfluence

1. Ipke Wachsmuth, "Gestures Offer Insight," *Scientific American Mind* 17, no. 5 (October 2006): 20–25, http://www.scientificamerican.com/article.cfm?id=gestures-offer-insight.

2. Frank Luntz, *Words That Work: It's Not What You Say, It's What People Hear* (New York: Hyperion, 2007).

3. Hamish Pringle and Peter Field, *Brand Immortality: How Brands Can Live Long and Prosper* (London: Konan Page, 2008).

Section 14: Brainfluence on the Web

1. Gitte Lindgaard et al., "Attention Web Designers: You Have 50 Milliseconds to Make a Good First Impression!" *Behavior and Information Technology* 25 no. 2 (March–April 2006): 115-126, http://www.ext.colostate.edu/conferences/ace-netc/lindgaard.pdf.

2. "Is the Beauty of a Sculpture in the Brain of the Beholder?" *ScienceDaily*, November 24, 2007, http://www.sciencedaily.com/releases/2007/11/071120201928.htm.

3. *One to One*; "Implications of User Engagement with Search Result Pages," in *One to One*, a blog by Jeremi Karnell, July 3, 2009, http://www.onetooneglobal.com/otocorporate-white-papers/2009/07/03/implications-of-user-engagement-with-search-result-pages-2/.

4. Luciano Gamberini et al., "Embedded Persuasive Strategies to Obtain Visitors' Data: Comparing Reward and Reciprocity in an Amateur, Knowledge-Based Website," *Lecture Notes in Computer Science* 4744 (2007): 187-198, http://www.springerlink.com/content/t3698286348v713n/.

5. Adam Gazzaley, "The Aging Brain: At the Crossroads of Attention and Memory," *User Experience* 8, no. 1 (1st Quarter 2009): 6-8, http://gazzaleylab.ucsf.edu/files/brain_ux81.pdf.

6. University of California San Francisco, "UCSF Study on Multitasking Reveals Switching Glitch in Aging Brain," news release, April 11, 2011, http://www.ucsf.edu/news/2011/04/9676/ucsf-study-multitasking-reveals-switching-glitch-aging-brain.

7. Dan Hill, *About Face: The Secrets of Emotionally Effective Advertising* (London: Kogan Page, 2010).

8. Steve Outing and Laura Rule, "The Best of Eyetrack III: What We Saw When We Looked Through Their Eyes," *Eyetrack III*, January 30, 2006, http://www.uvsc.edu/disted/decourses/dgm/2740/IN/steinja/lessons/05/docs/eyetrack_iii.pdf.

9. Clifford Nass, "Sweet Talking Your Computer," *Wall Street Journal*, August 28, 2010, http://online.wsj.com/article/SB1000142405274870395970457545341113 2636080.html.

Index

279